The Psychological Consequences of Crowding

The Psychological
Consequences
of Crowding

Uday Jain

Sage Publications
New Delhi / Newbury Park / London

Copyright © Uday Jain, 1987

First published in 1987 by

Sage Publications India Pvt Ltd
M-32 Greater Kailash Market I
New Delhi 110 048

Sage Publications Inc
2111 West Hillcrest Drive
Newbury Park, California 91320

Sage Publications Ltd
28 Banner Street
London EC1Y 8QE

Published under the authority of Bhopal University with financial assistance from the U.G.C. under publication grant.

Published by Tejeshwar Singh for Sage Publications India Pvt Ltd, photo-typeset by Printers Plates and printed at Chaman Offset Printers.

ISBN   0-8039-9546-6 (U.S.)
81-7036-075-7 (India)

Contents

List of Tables

List of Figures

Foreword

The population explosion in the contemporary world has posed a threat of high magnitude for planners and policy-makers. There is growing realisation that a balanced approach towards managing the available resources is essential for the growth and maintenance of a livable environment. In this context we need scientific understanding of the nature and consequences of phenomena like population and crowding.

The present research monograph by Dr Uday Jain is a significant attempt to analyse the behavioural consequences of spatial and social density. His research has convincingly demonstrated that the experience of crowding inside the home and external environment has adverse consequences for interpersonal attraction, affective functions and mental health. He has shown that the nature and consequences of crowding are culture specific. He draws our attention towards planning for human environment in congruence with the eco-cultural setting of behaviour.

I hope that this work will receive the attention of students of human behaviour, environmental experts and those who are involved in policy planning and implementation.

Bhopal   **M L Jain**
                                       Vice-Chancellor, Bhopal University

Preface

Modern man has achieved remarkable success in controlling his environment. Such an effort is clearly intended to transform environment to suit human needs. The impressive attainments of the West are held as models by Third World countries. The question of environmental planning and management was not examined within the framework of socio-cultural and ecological boundary conditions. Instead, the conditions prevailing in society were assessed according to the norms and scales of development accepted in the developed countries. This disregard of natural conditions has contributed to a considerable deterioration in the human environment. The experience of different types of pollution, population growth, crowding and climatic changes in developing countries like India seem to be linked with unmindful interventions in the process of environmental planning. This and many other social problems which the developing countries are facing need an interdisciplinary perspective, if they have to be analysed adequately in order to make human life better.

In this work, Dr Uday Jain has systematically applied social psychology in an area which deserves the attention of social scientists as well as planners. Dr Jain has treated the problem of crowding as that of environmental stress. In a series of interrelated studies he has empirically examined the diverse effects of crowding as well as the nature of crowding experiences. His work represents a well organised programme of applied social psychological research. He has integrated experimental as well as non-laboratory research approaches to examine the issues of need pattern, need intensity, mental health, and personal space. He has developed an interesting construct of competition tolerance which seems to have significance in studying not only crowding but a variety of social phenomena. The results of the present work indicate that social density and spatial density do not have one-to-one correspondence with the feeling of crowding. It has been systematically shown that the experience of crowding is related to specific individual variables. The findings at many points differ from those noted in western studies and implies that a culture-specific approach emphasising emics has more relevance in studying problems of applied nature.

The present work has largely been confined to characterising the experience and consequences of crowding. However, many suggestions are implicit in the findings for improving the quality of human environment. It is hoped that Dr Jain's future work will be related to the planning of a better environment. The present volume is an introduction to the psychology of crowding in India. It will definitely draw the attention of scholars and students interested in social problems in general and environmental problems in particular. I congratulate Dr Jain for undertaking this project.

The present volume is part of the ongoing research programme in Applied Social Psychology in the Department of Psychology at Bhopal University.

Bhopal   **Girishwar Misra**
                                           Professor and Head,
                                    Department of Psychology,
                            and Dean, School of Social Sciences,
                                            Bhopal University

Acknowledgements

To begin with, I am thankful to the Vice-Chancellor and members of the publication grant committee of Bhopal University, who very kindly recommended this work for the University Grants Commission's Publication Grant. Thanks are due to the authorities of the UGC, New Delhi.

The publication would not have been possible without the multifaceted help I got from Professor Girishwar Misra, Head, Department of Psychology, Bhopal University. Not only as a Professor but also as a friend I am grateful to him for his generous help.

I shall fail in my duty if I forget to thank my friends, colleagues, students and the authorities of the University of Rajasthan, Jaipur, where many of the studies reported here, were conducted. My students deserve appreciation for the help they rendered in conducting the studies. Some of these studies are the outcome of two research projects sponsored by the Indian Council of Social Science Research. I am grateful to the authorities of the ICSSR for funding these projects.

For the encouraging and critical comments on an earlier draft of the manuscript I thank Professors Janak Pandey and S.N. Upadhyaya and my teacher Professor H.S. Asthana.

Bhopal, December 1986   *Uday Jain*

– 1 –

Introduction

Modern man is experiencing an intense struggle for his existence. Developing as well as developed countries are confronted with poverty, war, violence, and crisis of energy of unprecedented magnitude. With some regional variations these problems are being faced by planners and policy-makers throughout the world and they are determining the social harmony and political stability of nations. While this situation is the outcome of a number of factors, population explosion emerges as one of the primary factors shaping the nature and extent of these problems. The growth of population has consequences for the individual, the social system, and the environment.

It is not an exaggeration to say that while human beings can produce diverse means for controlling the environment they have failed in attaining corresponding control over themselves. One of the major factors which has led to the unprecedented growth of population is lack of individual control. Also, at the individual level one rarely perceives the magnitude of the problem which exists at the national level.

Even after the best available motivational techniques and incentive systems were introduced success could not be achieved in bringing the rate of population growth to the desired level in most Third World countries. As a result, policy-makers, physical and social

scientists, and environmental experts, have all become concerned
with understanding the dynamics of population growth and its consequences for human life.

Population Growth

Our day-to-day experiences and general information about the consequences of rapid population growth have led us to believe that
growing world population has led to numerous problems and has
decreased the pleasures of personal and social life. It is now believed
that poverty, crime, delinquency, aggression, deindividuation, social
insecurity, and price rise, to name just a few of the problems, are
directly linked with the population explosion. It may be naive to
associate all these problems with population growth. But it is the only
scientific attitude which would enable us to understand the consequences of population growth and the ways of reducing its negative
consequences. Many authors have depicted a very depressing future
for mankind after assessing and projecting the extent of population
growth particularly in relation to the depletion of resources (Carter,
1969; Ganguli, 1974; Gupte, 1984; Toffler, 1970).

On the basis of the present growth rate the world's population is
predicted to be approximately 10.5 billion in 2110 A.D. Raghavachari
(1974) projected population growth in India on the basis of actual
population in 1971 (i.e., 546.9 million) for the year 1984. According
to this estimate, India's population in 1984 should have been 685.8
million. The 1981 Census records the total population around 685
million, which closely approximates the estimated population. This
suggests that more intensive efforts have to be made to arrest the
growth of population. In a country like India increasing population
growth will necessarily undermine the efforts of improving the
quality of life by spreading literacy, improving health services, and
providing housing and food (Brown, 1979). The United Nations
Report on Urbanisation (1968) has observed that in India 34 per cent
of the rural families, 44 per cent in urban areas, and 67 per cent in
big cities live in one room houses. The figures are much higher for
Calcutta where 79 per cent of the families live in one room. In addition, thousands of people are homeless and live on pavements. The

solution to these problems demands careful planning and effective implementation.

Granting our limitations in bringing down the growth rate the only alternative left is the proper planning of manpower, of the living environment, conservation of resources, and exploration of new resources. In this context perhaps a clear understanding of the human consequences of high population density, high growth rate, and of rapid urbanisation is warranted. It is perhaps with this view that Swamy (1974) could visualise the positive side of high population when he suggested the benefits of population growth for accelerated economic development in India. The basic points of such arguments cannot be ignored since in many developing countries both human potential and natural resources have not yet been adequately exploited and planning has never been geared in the direction of optimum utilisation of available manpower in different spheres.

In order to plan the alternatives for proper utilisation of manpower or physical resources, the influences of different characteristics of population on human life have to be carefully investigated. The role of social scientists in this context is important because questions pertaining to population growth, to a large extent, are questions of social life. Scientific theories on population have to provide insights into how and why population characteristics are responsible for human functioning in society.

Along with the growth of population every society has to adapt itself to the changing situations. To this end three alternative strategies have been suggested, namely, a real expansion, adoption of technological and social innovations, and population control. Psychologists ask how and why an individual's behaviour is affected by different sizes and types of population. At an empirical level the psychologist's task is difficult as he wishes to explore the relationships between different characteristics of population (viz., size, density, composition), and individual's behaviour. However, the relationship between these two sets of variables becomes complex because of the confounding of several variables. Population growth has resulted in pollution, excessive demands for food, depletion of natural resources and damage to the quality of life (Lazarus, 1974, p. 101). The psychologist's task, therefore, is to find out how and in what ways all these concomitants of population growth affect social and personal behaviour of individuals. As Fawcett (1970) has rightly suggested that psychological studies of individual level consequences of population growth might point out the ways towards social arrangement.

Recent studies have shown a number of problems associated with excessive population growth. These problems seem to be interlinked. For example, the mere presence of a large number of people in a small space creates a feeling of crowding which may, in turn, lead to tension and irritation. This may result in broken homes, social disintegration, and loss of financial support to the dependants, less care for children, etc. In an overcrowded home parents may be forced to ignore their wards who, in turn, may perceive their home to be a relatively unattractive place. They may, therefore, seek refuge from their home to their peer groups and may even engage in socially undesirable activities.

Population growth is thus not exclusively the growth in the size of the population, but also the density of population within a limited space. Moreover, technological and industrial development has lured people to metropolitan towns for employment, education and the enjoyment of modern facilities. The growth also includes size, density and heterogeneity. Thus these concomitants of population growth together influence human behaviour.

Selecting any particular behaviour at a given time and then attempting to find out its antecedents in population characteristics may create difficulty as several other characteristics of population may intervene and influence the behaviour in question. This type of problem is very general in psychological research where man-environment interaction is the aim of investigation. This problem is partly solved in controlled experimental studies in laboratories, which have their own limitations as their findings cannot be generalised to real life situations. Well controlled studies on the effects of population characteristics in general, and population density in particular, have been carried out on animals and will be discussed later. Their conclusions, however, can hardly be generalised to human populations. However, despite the methodological and practical limitations psychologists have been trying to bring out the behavioural effects of crowding.

Density: Physical Crowding

A difficulty which often arises in the study of relationship between population density and behaviour is concerned with the definition or nature of the particular population characteristic in question. High density or overcrowding may not be stressful in itself but as a component of the stress complex comprising of noise, pollution, reduced personal space, industrialisation, etc., it may be treated as an aversive situation. This contention has been expressed in a somewhat different context, by Freedman (1972) and opposed by others (Marshall and Heslin, 1975). Moreover, similar densities may have different effects on human behaviour in different cultural settings, in developed and developing countries and across different socio-economic strata.

The main problem which arises in verifying these hypotheses is concerned with matching the two samples of different population having similar density. Only laboratory studies would be able to control the relevant variables or to equate the two groups to be compared. However, their conclusions may not be generalised to real living conditions. The inherent difficulties involved in generalising from laboratory setting to larger population necessitates another approach. Statistical procedure of partial correlation is ideally suited for obtaining the differential effects of many concomitant variables which cannot be controlled in a field study. Some efforts have been made in this direction but the results are still inconclusive (Davis, 1971; Kannampuzha, 1976; Mehrabian and Russell, 1974; Winsborough, 1965).

Theoretically, size and density characteristics of population in a limited space stratify a society in various segments and dictate the economic and social relations among the members. However, density-behaviour relationship will also be a function of the type of density being investigated. A given level of population density in a community area may be achieved by any one or different combinations of the following four components of the density—number of persons per room, number of rooms per housing unit, number of houses per residential structure, and number of residential structures per residential ward.

Most of the studies on density have been done on urban samples. However, density may also vary in rural areas. It will be interesting to know whether high density in rural areas has similar effects as in urban areas. Because of varied experiences and a large population, individuals in urban areas sense a loss of identity. Proshansky (1973) has rightly pointed out the ill effects of crowding in urban life which seem to transform human beings into simple machines. Milgram (1970) observes three common characteristics of city life—large number of people, high density, and heterogeneity of population. Thus crowding has been regarded as a chief characteristic of urban life. Despite the variation in the characteristics of urban and rural population the condition of high and low density in its relative sense also exists in rural areas.

In India as well as in other developing countries high population density is correlated with scarce resources (physical as well as economic). It is therefore highly probable that it will influence behaviour negatively. Although the rate of population growth and population density in India has become alarming, a systematic study of the behavioural aspects of crowding has not received the attention of researchers for a long time (Pandey, 1978). India has an annual growth rate of 2.4 per cent. The average density of population in India is estimated at 216 persons per km^2 (Census, 1981), of course wider variations are observed in different states, viz., 4194 persons per km^2 in Delhi to 100 persons per km^2 in Rajasthan. Even the average density of household at 549.53 per km^2 in urban areas is quite high. With a population of 685 million and poor economic and physical resources Indians are under high pressure of competitive situations in a rapidly advancing world.

In the psychological study of population growth attention has been paid on two counts. First, density is relatively easily manipulable in controlled conditions, and second, high density living conditions can produce stress and negative effects on social behaviours. Saegert (1978) has presented an extensive review of psychological research on density and concluded that the relationship of density with the feeling of aggression and other negative behaviours are not unequivocal. In fact the differences in the results of various studies can be attributed to the type of density which has been incorporated, such as social and spatial density. Social density consists of a comparison of different sized groups in the same space, i.e., if one goes on increasing the number of persons in a given space then high social density can be attained. On the other hand, if we vary space size and keep the number of persons constant then we find spatial density increasing along with the reduction in space size. The two types of density may lead to differential effects on behaviour (Altman, 1978; McGrew, 1970). Another distinction has been made between inside and outside density. A large number of people living in a small dwelling is referred to as high inside density whereas a large number of people in the neighbourhood is high outside density (Jain, 1984; Zlutnick and Altman, 1972).

Apart from these variations in density several situational factors including the nature of tasks involved in the density conditions may create differences in the effects of density (Freedman, Brisky and Cavoukian, 1980). Psychological models have offered various explanations of high density effects on behaviour. For example, it has been suggested that the presence of a large number of people in a smaller space creates attentional overload because of which people express their inability to process the incoming information (Cohen, 1978) and experience stress. Also, high density may produce negative effects because of loss of control over social situations (Aiello, Epstein and Karlin, 1975; Altman, 1975; Saegert, 1973).

The Feeling of Crowding

There is consensus among researchers that crowding deals with the subjective state which typically has a stress component. It is associated with the perception of reduced physical and/or psychological space. Feeling of discomfort, perception of the loss of control over social interaction, encroachment on privacy, negative perception of the space, boredom, etc., are considered as characteristic features of the feeling of crowding. Thus this feeling is a perceptual-affective state of stress which leads to negative behavioural consequences. This demands new coping strategies to reduce the feeling of crowding. Although the various components of crowding have been used indiscriminately in research, it is generally agreed that the feeling of crowding is a negative psychological state. Sundstrom (1975) has viewed the feeling as a sequential process in which conditions of high density may lead to the feeling of crowding depending upon certain personal and situational conditions.

The research on crowding now occupies a salient position in environmental psychology. The chief concern of current research is with specifying the conditions leading to crowding. As Stokols (1978b, p. 272) has rightly commented 'the assumption that crowding involves a reduction of personal control over the environment is central in psychological analysis but the conditions under which reduced spatial or social controls are most salient have not been identified.' The crucial problem of research, therefore, is to investigate the specific factors of high density which determine the differential effects of objective crowding and the corresponding subjective state.

Theoretical Models

The distinction between high population density and crowding has led investigators to formulate models specifying the antecedents and consequences of the feeling of crowding. In this endeavour several theoretical models have been proposed (Stokols, 1976). A brief description of these and other models seems to be in order.

Stimulus Overload Model

This model proposes high density as a stressor because of its potential to provide excessive stimulation to the individual (e.g., Baum, Davis, Calesnick and Gathel, 1982; Desor, 1972; Saegert, 1973; Valins and Baum, 1973). Since individuals receive additional stimuli which they cannot handle, they experience crowding which may lead to confusion at the cognitive level, fatigue at the physical level, and escape and withdrawal at the behavioural level. This line of thinking led Cohen (1978) to formulate a model of environmental stress which states that stressors reduce the amount of attention available for other tasks. The individual in the stressful environment pays attention only to some cues and is forced to ignore others. This model seems to be adequate for explaining some environmental stressors. However, density situation is a peculiar stress situation where many social and normative factors operate along with the presence of other people (Saegert, 1978). Instead of attentional overload high density situation can be considered as a situation of overload in which people may develop various strategies to deal with unwanted, unpredictable, and unavoidable interference from others.

Behavioural Constraints Model

It visualises high density as a stressor because it imposes restriction on behavioural freedom (Proshansky, Ittelson and Rivlin, 1970; Stokols, 1972). If under high density an individual feels reduced behavioural freedom he may experience psychological reactance and infringement which may lead to withdrawal or improved interpersonal relationship. An extension of this model is the loss of control model as suggested by Rodin (1976), according to which presence of a large number of people in a relatively small area generates the feeling that the individual's control over the situation is reduced. He may try to gain control, failing which he may experience helplessness (Burger, Oakman and Bullard, 1983).

Ecological Model

From this perspective high density is considered disruptive to the extent that it leads to the scarcity of social roles and physical resources (e.g., Wicker and Kirmeyer, 1977). Citing the work of Gibson (1977) on perception of objects, Baron and Mendel (1978) recommended an ecological analysis of high density effects. They have argued that the concept of *affordance* can be used as social affordance for the analysis of high density effects. Affordance has been defined in terms of the functional properties of objects which possibly can be encountered by an active organism interacting with the environment. These investigators have tried to use ecological analysis to understand behaviour under high density in dormitory settings. Density effects can be considered in terms of impact on recognition and utilisation of affordances.

The ecological orientation emphasises the architectural as well as the social aspects of the human environment. As the group size in a given space increases the affordances within the environment may change depending upon the ability of the person perceiving such structural environments.

A variant of the ecological model can be noted in the typology of crowding experiences given by Stokols (1978a). He feels that the experience of crowding includes the perception of lack of control over the environment and a desire to transform psychological or physical space to gain more control. To determine the persistence and intensity of crowding Stokols (1978a) has, suggested two dimensions, i.e., thwarting and environment. Thwarting can be of two types—neutral and personal. Neutral thwarting includes unintentional annoyances stemming from social or non-social environments. Personal thwartings are intentionally imposed on the individual by other persons The former is exemplified in the situation of congested residential rooms where one has to share limited facilities, and the latter in the case of intentional disturbances created by others. The intensity of crowding will depend on the individual's ability to reduce thwartings.

Environmental settings have been categorised into two types—primary and secondary. House, classroom, and work place are examples of primary environment, where persons meet each other for important tasks. The secondary environment includes recreation centres and transportation centres, etc., where persons meet others for shorter durations. High density will be more disruptive in primary environments. The model further predicts differential consequences in environments differing on the aforesaid dimensions.

Attribution Model

Worchel (1978) has proposed that high density is more likely to create a condition where there is violation of personal space. In this situation if the individual attributes his arousal because of personal space encroachment to others, only then he would feel a sense of crowding otherwise not. Thus the feeling of crowding results from attribution. The focus of the individual's attention may shift when he is in a high density situation and the nature of this shift determines whether the feeling of crowding is experienced. Worchel, Brown and

Webb (1983) have suggested the importance of attribution of stress to high density, as a determinant of the feeling of crowding and its negative effects.

Pointing out the limitations of the first three models, Stokols (1978a) has emphasised a crucial antecedent of the feeling of crowding, i.e., the desire to increase space or distance between oneself and others. He further elaborated the environment as primary and secondary and the thwarting dimension of crowding as natural and personal. The antecedents and consequences of high density will then vary with the 2×2 fold combinations of environment and thwarting dimensions. The elaborated model, of course, predicts a more specific relationship between antecedents and consequences of crowding experiences but needs more empirical support.

Stress and Arousal Model

Arousal has been considered as an important physiological dimension of stress. The theoretical analysis and experimental work relating stress and arousal (Berlyne, 1960, 1971; Hebb, 1972; Kahneman, 1973) have generally evinced an inverted U-shaped relationship between stressors (i.e., complex task) and arousal. This relationship is, however, mediated by a number of psychological and situational variables (Glass and Singer, 1972). There is also evidence of adaptation to stress.

Evans (1978) has reviewed the research on arousal and spatial behaviour. He has noted that high density or invasion of personal space does cause decrement in task performance. The physiological measures of arousal such as blood pressure, skin conductance and cortisone level have been reported under high density conditions. Thus evidence is available to support that crowding and invasion of personal space are stressors which lead to high arousal.

Evans (1978) has also noted general difficulties and contradictory evidence against the arousal model. These include disassociations of somatic and behavioural arousal with psycho-physiological indices, simultaneous presence of opposite autonomic responses, and lack of straightforward explanation of after-effects. Evans (1978) concluded that whenever physical space is reduced beyond a certain level individuals experience increased arousal leading to stress.

Despite these theoretical and empirical efforts, the question of specific aspects of high density (physical crowding) which produce a feeling of crowding (psychological crowding) and behavioural disturbances is still controversial. The controversy seems partly due to the complex nature of the variable (i.e., density). The question of optimal density poses additional complexity in the sense that theoretically, it seems possible to obtain a threshold of density above which it will have negative effects, but in practice any threshold cannot be generalised. In addition to the nature of density the question of its relationship with the feeling of crowding is not very clear. We do not know the necessary and sufficient causes of the feeling of crowding. Having moved from the sociological tradition to the ethological tradition and on to the social-psychological tradition, research has now reached a stage where reformulation of the concepts, as well as methodological innovations are necessary (Altman, 1978).

Research on Crowding: An Overview

Effects of crowding on behavioural aspects have been extensively investigated, particularly in the last two decades, because of their theoretical and applied importance in human settlements. It has been predicted that we are fast approaching a time when solitude will be rare because of social encroachment by a rapidly increasing population. The relevant studies have been reviewed elsewhere (Sundstrom, 1978; Pandey, 1978).

The present overview covers research in the following areas: animal performance, human behaviour, health and stress. Animal studies have historical importance as they have generated the interest of psychologists to look into the problems of crowding at a human level. These studies are still continuing because animal population can be subjected to rigorous control required by experimental research. Finally, animal studies have the advantage of generating and testing hypotheses about interventions and their effects which would be unethical to carry out with human subjects. The performance studies have investigated the effects of crowding and called upon a lot of controversies on the negative-positive effects of crowding. Studies dealing with the behavioural consequences of crowding are related to the short as well as long-term effects and have significance for the general theory of behaviour. Health related problems of crowding have an applied value for they are related to human wellbeing. In the last category the studies have been related to a much debated issue with theoretical as well as applied implications: In what way can crowding be considered as an environmental stress?

Animal Studies

Initial studies on crowding were conducted on animals. Christian, Flyger and Davis (1960) observed a herd of deer whose population rose and eventually exceeded the normal density. Despite abundance of food and absence of disease, a massive death rate was recorded. An examination of the dead animals revealed prolonged hyperactivity of the adrenals. Therefore, the investigators concluded that death was due to stress reactions. In another study Christian (1959) examined both tame and wild mice and found that increasing population density produced hypertrophy of the adrenals and atrophy of the gonads.

Calhoun (1962) conducted experimental studies on animals on the assumption that their implications may be applied to other organisms including homosapiens. He used the term 'Behavioural Sink' to refer to the gross distortions of behaviour that he observed in his experiment on rats. He partitioned a 10' × 14' room into four pens using an electrified partition which had ramps built over it so that the rats could go from one pen to another. The number two and three pens tended to have a higher population density than pens one and four. The female members of the population gradually distributed themselves about equally in the four pens, while the male population was concentrated in the middle two pens. Each corner pen contained a dominant male who could tolerate a few other males if they respected his dominance. Soon bizzarre behaviour began to develop, particularly among animals in the crowded middle pens. The females in the densely populated pens became less efficient in building nests, and ultimately quit building them. Calhoun (1962) pointed out that the aggressive and dominant males, the most normal in that population, displayed abnormal behaviour on some occasions, e.g., they would attack females, were juvenile, and were less active. Very unusual behaviour such as biting the tails of other rats was frequently observed. Hall's (1966) research also evinced social disorganisation, excessive aggression and massive death rate due to the adverse effects of crowding in the animal colonies. Carson's (1969) review also supported the hypothesis that 'crowding' in animal and human populations produces physiological stress reaction known as 'General Adaptation Syndrome'.

Similarly Dubos (1965) has shown, as reported by Heimstra and McDonald (1973), that the effects of crowding produce susceptibility to 'crowd diseases'. They hypothesised that crowding affects tissue responses by decreasing its resistance to infection. In one investigation mice were infected with a standard dose of 'trichinella' and then were either isolated in individual jars or caged in groups immediately after infection. Fifteen days later when these mice were examined it was found that all the grouped animals had large number of worms in their intestines, whereas only three out of twelve of the isolated group displayed any sign of infection. Although exposure to infection had been identical, apparently, the crowding effect had increased the ability of the parasite to invade the intestinal wall. In natural habitat woodchucks were found with consistent morphological modifications in crowding conditions (Snyder, 1961).

Many studies on animals (e.g., Calhoun, 1971, 1973; Christian, 1955, 1963; Davis, 1971) have shown that the population size of many mammalian species is self limiting, i.e., after the population reaches a certain density it tends to stabilise regardless of the amount of available food. Stress leads to physiological changes such as increased adrenal size, reduced gonadal activity and a consequent reduction in the rate of reproduction. Goeckner, Greenough and Mead (1973) reared rats in different densities. They found that rats reared under crowded environment showed poor performance on complex tasks but on simple tasks the effect of density was not observed.

Aforesaid studies have shown that crowding leads to stress reactions in animals and consequently the animal population stabilises or gradually declines. Furthermore, these studies have shown the behavioural, performance as well as physiological ill effects of crowding.

Whether these effects can be generalised to human population is a debatable question. Freedman (1979) commented that 'in explaining the effects of density we need not posit different mechanism for people and other animals' (p.81). On the other hand, Baron and Needel (1980), considering human cognitive and social competencies, have argued for very limited and cautious generalisation of the effects of crowding from animals to human beings. It seems appropriate, as will be evident from the following review, that crowding effects are complex and evidence on cognitive control in human beings do not allow such generalisations.

Human Studies

BEHAVIOURAL CONSEQUENCES OF CROWDING: What does an individual do in a high density situation? How does he feel? Why does he feel as he does? Does high density lead to the feeling of crowding and negative consequences for behaviour? Although the answers to these questions are not definitive, nonetheless, our understanding regarding the consequences of crowding has advanced considerably. There is a general consensus among researchers that high population density does not always lead to negative effects, rather it may create positive feelings under certain situations, for example, watching a cricket match is enjoyed in the midst of a huge crowd. The negative effects of density are mediated by several non-spatial factors and psychological mechanisms.

Research on human beings, in most cases, have not investigated the unconfounded effects of high density on human behaviour because of methodological limitations and of non-availability of pure density. Whenever density is created in a laboratory situation, it loses its natural flavour and the participants remain aware explicitly or implicitly about the purpose of the present condition, which in most cases remains a temporary affair. In realistic high dense conditions the confounding of other factors such as type of interaction, level of adaptation and tolerance of crowded living may occur. Despite these limitations our knowledge of the mechanisms and consequences of crowding has advanced.

EFFECTS ON SOCIAL BEHAVIOUR: Crowding is a social situation in the sense that people have to interact or to avoid interactions. Studies on the effects of high density on social behaviour, by and large, have revealed the negative effects. Even in conditions where people anticipate high density they show reduced liking for their fellow beings, lesser interpersonal attraction and limited interaction as compared to the persons anticipating low density.

Baum and Greenberg (1975) asked their subjects to wait in a room where more persons (high density) were expected to arrive. Similarly in a low density condition only a few persons were expected to come. It was found that subjects who were anticipating high density expressed greater feeling of crowding and discomfort, lesser liking for the fellows waiting with them, seated farther away from others, preferred seats in corners, and noticed others less than those who were anticipating low density. Similar findings on the effects of anticipating high spatial and social density along with sex differences were obtained by Baum and Koman (1976). The negative effects were greater for males than for females, in relation to same sex confederates waiting with them. However, these results are not confirmed in relation with performance data in actual crowding (Klein and Harris, 1979).

Sex and group composition as well as space and group size were manipulated in a laboratory study in order to see their effects on interpersonal attraction, liking for the group as a whole and feeling in general (Marshall and Heslin, 1975). The results showed that mixed sex groups exposed to high density reported positive emotions. The findings did not support the expected negative effects. Perhaps many factors other than density are responsible for the presumed negative effects. Worchel (1978), for instance, has identified one such factor— the attribution of discomfort to the presence of others in high density. This factor is found to be responsible for low interpersonal attraction. Griffitt and Veitch (1971) in an experimental study found significant negative effects of high density and high temperature on mood, liking for the room and experiment.

In a number of field studies high density was found to be associated with lower frequencies of interaction (e.g., Hutt and Vaizcy, 1966; Loo, 1972; Price, 1971; Wolfe, 1975). Even the debilitating effects on non-verbal behaviours such as eye contact, facial regard, and compensatory gestures have been observed (Argyle and Dean, 1965; Patterson, 1973; Sundstrom, 1975).

Munroe and Munroe (1972) investigated the effects of very high and rapidly increasing population density on affective relationship and attitudes in three tribal societies of East Africa, varying in population density. The dependent measures applied were holding of hands, short-term memory of affiliative words, and semantic differential evaluation of family roles. It was noted that the residents of high density held hands less often. It was found that tribals under high density evaluated their family members somewhat negatively as compared to the tribal residents of low density areas.

Booth (1976) conducted a large survey in Toronto (Canada) and reported lower contacts with neighbours, relatives in subjective as well as objective crowding conditions. Females were found more reserved than males. However, both showed lesser contact in high density conditions.

Recent studies on college dormitories have observed adverse effects on social behaviour, particularly on relationship with room mates, and interaction with neighbours (e.g., Aiello and Capriglione, 1975; Aiello and Baum, 1979; Baron, Mendel, Adams and Griffen, 1976; Lavin, 1983). Aiello, Baum and Gormley (1981) further noted that in a college dormitory situation students living in triple rooms felt more crowded, showed lesser attraction to room mates, greater social tensions, and negative emotions than residents of a double room.

Under high density situation the mere sight of too many people stimulates and provokes some people. Tucker and Friedman (1972) have suggested that with increasing population density males tend to gather in similar and thus limited groups than females. It appears that as density rises the amount of interaction between persons decreases. Reduction of interaction seems to occur as a psychological consequence of stress. With increased population density there is a corresponding increase in unavoidable intrusive interpersonal encounter.

The results of these studies can hardly be generalised to natural life settings (Desor, 1972; Stokols, 1972; Rapaport, 1975). Some field experiments have been conducted in dormitories using student samples (Aiello, Voutier, and Bernstein, 1983). However, dormitories provide a special type of situation where strangers come and stay for a short duration.

The significance of spatial privacy in residential settings was evident in an early study done in Chicago (Galle, Gove and McPherson, 1972). It was found that those living in areas with dwellings averaging fewer rooms per person showed increased use of community mental health facilities. Cohen, Glass and Phillips (1979) noted that residential crowding with strangers (in institutions) is experienced more negatively than crowding with a family household. This indicates that the nature of social relationship among the residents is a more important determinant of the impact of inside population density.

WITHDRAWAL AND CROWDING: Another behaviour pattern which has been investigated extensively in crowding research is withdrawal. Withdrawal presupposes the aversiveness of the situation because of potential threat, or because of low capabilities to meet the demands of the situation, or because of interpersonal conflicts. Since high density has been found to lower interpersonal attraction and to a dislike for the place it produces withdrawal response in human beings under high density.

The studies on interaction are relevant here in the sense that low interaction under high density manifests withdrawal from social situations due to crowding stress. Similarly compensatory reactions in terms of decreasing signs of immediacy also represent withdrawal reactions (Sundstrom, 1978). From the point of social contact it appears that withdrawal is associated with the level of social contact (Baum and Valins, 1977; Valins and Baum, 1973). Another view of withdrawal has been reflected in studies where subjects showed their inability to participate in the subsequent experiments under high social density conditions (e.g., Dooley, 1974). This represents avoidance from similar stressful situations. Many studies have been conducted on the relationship between crowding and aggression (Freedman, Levy, Buchanan and Price, 1972).

In addition Mehrabian and Russell (1974) used the desire to leave and avoidance to explore in the described environmental situation. They found that these measures are not always correlated with crowding and suggested the use of separate measures for studying approach-avoidance behaviour in a given situation. However, most of the researcners have perceived withdrawal as avoidance of interaction. Baldassare (1975) could not find any relationship between household density and withdrawal. The overall results do not yield unequivocal support for the hypothesis that high density and withdrawal are positively related. Perhaps the inevitability of the stress situation and the availability of alternative goals, perceived importance of the situation, and personality factors may mediate the effects of high density on withdrawal. In view of the possibility of some mediators and common observations in the Indian context, withdrawal from social interaction cannot be expected. Indians believe in honouring guests and irrespective of the degree of density people generally maintain social contacts with neighbours, relatives, friends and others. Still there is the possibility of withdrawal in high density situations in terms of the desire to leave, escape from competitive situations, and shifting affiliation from one group to another. In view of the fact that withdrawal responses from high density situations are multidimensional, socio-cultural factors have to be taken into consideration while assessing the degree of withdrawal, or from generalisation of findings from one density situation to another. However, withdrawal responses are observed even in different cultural settings (Altman and Chemers, 1980; Schmidt, 1983).

EFFECTS ON HELPING: Prosocial behaviour has also been considered as a potential influence of high density. It has been observed in a number of investigations that greater density leads to less amount of helping (Brickman, Teger, Gabrielle, McLaughlin, Berger and Sunday, 1973). The comparison of urban-rural residents for helping behaviour, for example, the use of a phone, correct overpayments, and report of theft, have been found less frequently among urban dwellers (e.g., Preet and Jain, 1986; Weiner, 1976). Darley and Latane (1968) have found that helping behaviour is readily observed in the case of a single bystander on the side of the victim rather than a group of bystanders. These investigators have suggested the concept of diffusion of responsibility to explain the apathy shown in case of emergency by a group of bystanders as every one in the group thinks that someone else will help the victim. The phenomenon of bystander apathy has been confirmed by Milgram (1977) who observed that willingness to allow a needy individual into one's house to use the telephone was higher in a smaller than in a larger city.

Another explanation of reduced helping in high density comes from a study by Konecni, Libuser, Morton and Ebbesen (1975) who showed that spatial invasions reduced the likelihood of helping the invader. In their study the invader (confederate) maintained a particular distance from pedestrians and dropped a pencil, acting as if unknowingly the pencil dropped. It was observed that closer the distance between the invader and the pedestrian lesser the chance that the pedestrian will inform or hand over the pencil. Since in crowd situations interpersonal distance is reduced the chances of helping others are also likely to be reduced. These studies indicate the reduction of helping in high density. However, the results are not consistent (House and Wolf, 1978; Korte and Kerr, 1975; Weiner, 1976). Studies on the effects of crowding on other prosocial behaviours such as donating, sharing, giving care and cooperation, have not received the attention of researchers in the field.

AGGRESSION AND CROWDING: Many studies have been conducted on the relationship between crowding and aggression. However, the findings are equivocal. Psychological theories on aggression generally predict a positive relationship between high density and aggression. Hutt and Vaizey (1966) reported increased aggression in high density and Loo (1972) observed the reverse effect. Price (1971) did not observe any effects of spatial density on aggression. All these studies were conducted on children's samples. The evidence of moderator effects comes from Rohe and Patterson's (1974) study They found a very high degree of aggression in the high density-low toys condition. This indicates the role of scarcity of valued resources in high density conditions for negative effects on behaviour such as aggression.

Even under high density situations, the aggressive responses differ in males and females. Stokols, Rall, Pinner and Schopler (1973) studied same sex groups in large and small groups and found that males rated themselves as more aggressive in small rooms than females. Females, however, rated themselves more aggressive in large rooms. Sundstrom (1975) studied male groups in high or low spatial density conditions and blocked their goals by interrupting them during task accomplishment. This study suggests another moderator, i.e., goal blocking as responsible for irritation and not density *per se.* More careful studies on aggression and crowding are needed to resolve the existing contradictions. These studies will have to look into other concomitants along with density and the feeling of crowding. In fact available theoretical models make contradictory predictions about high density and aggression. For example, the arousal model would predict a positive relationship since high density is supposed to induce arousal and arousal has been found to be related to aggression. On the other hand, the concept of loss of control would predict withdrawal, rather than aggression, as the most probable response to high density situations (Paulus, 1980). Thus both theoretical and empirical contradictions are yet to be resolved.

In addition to aggression, crowding also results in responses representing hostility. Zeedyk-Ryan and Smith (1983) required their subjects to remain in high-low density conditions for 18 hours as a part of their field training in Disaster and Civil Defence Course. The subjects in the high social density situation marked greater number of adjectives on Affect Adjective Check List which expressed hostility, compared to their counterparts in the low social density condition. The two groups, however, did not differ in their responses on adjectives expressing anxiety. This study supported Worchel and Teddlie's attribution model (1976) in the sense that the knowledge that others were in a low density situation produced hostile responses in subjects in a high density situation.

EFFECTS OF CROWDING ON TASK PERFORMANCE: If crowding is considered as stress then it must interfere with task performance. The famous Yerkes-Dodson Law also states that arousal will lead to decrement in performance on complex tasks, but will facilitate performance on simple tasks. Even the concept of control predicts that performance on complex tasks would be negatively affected by high density.

The findings on task performance under crowding condition are, however, not consistent. Some early studies used simple tasks and showed no effect of high density on performance (e.g., Bergman, 1971; Fagot and Patterson, 1969; Freedman, Klevansky and Ehrlich, 1971; Rawls, Trego, McGaffery and Rawls, 1972; Stokols et al., 1973). Some support of the Yerkes-Dodson Law has been accumulated in recent years (e.g., Dooley, 1974; McClelland, 1974; Paulus and Matthews, 1980; Saegert, 1974) and the negative effect on complex task performance has been reported. For instance, Sherrod (1974) found negative effects even on simple tasks, however, under the choice condition, which provided perceived control, the effect was lesser than under the no choice condition.

In a college dormitory situation, Aiello, Epstein and Karlin (1975) have found evidence of performance decrements on a complex task over time in overcrowded conditions as compared to less crowded dormitories. On the lines suggested in the learned helplessness model (Seligman, 1975), Rodin (1976) found no difference between children from low and high density housing units as far as learning was concerned, but, when a 'switching key' for controlling contingencies was introduced performance decreased as a function of density.

Evans (1978) has extensively reviewed studies on task performance and has outlined the difficulties involved in drawing conclusions on the effects of crowding on task performance. For example, considering crowding as a stress condition producing arousal, support for the above mentioned studies showing decrement of performance on a complex task is obtained. However, where crowding has not had any effect on either a complex or a simple task (e.g., Epstein and Karlin, 1975; Freedman *et al.*, 1971) ,it might be due to the nature of the tasks employed in those studies. If a task does not overload the information processing system it may not produce immediate stress effects (Cohen, 1978; Glass and Singer, 1972). Thus, the level of task difficulty is determined not only by the time taken to complete a task but also by the amount of load it puts on the individual's information processing capacity.

Langer and Saegert (1977) tested the effects of high density in a field setting on complex cognitive and behavioural tasks hypothesising lowered efficiency in high density. They also hypothesised that if prior information about the aversive effects of crowding is provided to the subjects it would enhance their control over the situation and would increase their efficiency. The subjects were required to select the more economical products from a given grocery list during crowded or uncrowded hours at a supermarket. These hypotheses were supported by the results and were explained in terms of attentional overload. McCallum, Rusbult, Hong, Walden and Schopler (1979) have emphasised the importance of behavioural goal as a determinant of the effect of crowding on task performance. If goals are important, individuals will maintain task performance at the cost of increasing stress.

These studies, thus, suggest that task performance depends upon multiple factors and crowding conditions are not solely responsible. In addition to the task and situation variables, individual variables are also found to be important while assessing the impact of crowding stress on task performance. More studies are needed to assess the interactive effects of these variables.

CROWDING AND HEALTH HAZARDS: The studies on social behaviour in general, and interpersonal interactions in particular, tend to suggest that persons living in high density conditions for prolonged periods may develop mental as well as physical health problems. Furthermore, even adaptation to environmental stress situations supposedly involves some psychological costs. This view also supports the contention that crowding must be related to pathological conditions. A casual reflection on the Indian societal conditions reveals that crowded homes are usually those where people cannot afford to live in bigger houses. A large number of slums in this country face the problem of high density. Similarly older colonies or areas of Indian cities are characterised by 'high inside and outside density.' The majority of the population in these areas is comprised of low and middle social class families. Thus crowding and poverty, or shortage of various spatial and non-spatial resources are related to high density living. Prolonged exposure to these living conditions is likely to produce detrimental effects on health of the residents. If, however, there is a higher incidence of disease in these localities it cannot be inferred that crowding is associated with poor health; though it is possible that crowding is responsible for uncleanliness, pollution and noise, which in turn is associated with poor health status.

Like other potential negative consequences of crowding many studies have provided evidence of poor health in urban environments, college dormitories, and prisons (McCain, Cox, Paulus, Luke and Abadzi, 1985). In a survey of Toronto city, Booth (1976) studied samples of children from low and high household density conditions. The health measures included presence of disease, body weight and height and physiological indicators of stress. The results showed certain adverse effects of crowded households on the physical development of children. Interestingly, he also found that parental health and socio-economic status are better predictors of children's health than household crowding.

In the same study, Booth (1976) examined adult samples, and

found objective household crowding to be positively related to six measures of stress for males and four for females. The Overall effects were small in magnitude and showed that crowded household conditions are stressful for men but not for women. Objective neighbourhood congestion had a tendency to reduce physiological resistance to stress.

In a review of studies on the association of crowding with poor health Sundstrom (1978) reported five studies supporting a positive association between high dwelling density or the feeling of crowding and ill health. Freedman, Heshka and Levy (1975) found no relationship between household density and indicators of ill health while others (Levy and Herszog, 1974) found an inverse relationship between the rate of hospital admissions and household density. Galle *et al.* (1972) reported positive correlation between high inside density and mortality.

Some recent studies have reported evidence of adverse consequences of living in high density conditions (see Cox, Paulus, McCain and Karlovac, 1982). McCain, Cox and Paulus (1980) observed a reduction in illness complaints as a result of segmenting the prisoners' dormitories in cubicles. Prisoners living in crowded housing units were found to have a higher number of complaints of illness (Cox, Paulus, McCain and Karlovac, 1982). Paulus, McCain and Cox (1978) observed increased death rate among psychiatric prisoners.

The negative effects of crowding on health are consistent with the arousal model of crowding which predicts that a higher level of arousal would result in low tolerance for frustration, discomfort, distress, negative mood, and increased pulse rate in crowded subjects (Karlin and Epstein, 1979). However, the arousal model fails to explain the findings which do not indicate a positive relationship between illness and high density. Probably Abramson, Seligman and Teasdale's (1978) attribution model of learned helplessness, which emphasises the importance of perceived loss of control over situations and attribution of responsibility of failure to internal factors, may provide a better explanation of the inconsistent findings. Perhaps it is the failure of perception of helplessness in crowding conditions and attribution to external factors, rather than internal causes of loss of control, which guard people from ill health, particularly from mental illness. However, direct evidence on this issue is not available.

A few studies have reported a significant relationship between anxiety and crowding (e.g., Bruch and Walker,1978). Iwata (1979) has reported a positive association of neuroticism with the experience of crowding. However, Kirmeyer (1978) in a review of relevant studies concluded that aggregate urban density had little effect on pathology independent of the socio-economic variables.

A sociological study was conducted in Chicago to determine the pathological effects of crowding in the home. The investigators (Gove, Hughes and Galle, 1979) examined a large sample and found that both objective as well as subjective crowding were strongly related to poor mental health. Studies which viewed the admission in mental hospitals as an index of mental health found that it was related to crowding (Bain, 1974; Levy and Herzog, 1974). On the contrary, other studies did not find any relationship between these variables (Golson, 1976; Richard, 1977). Mitchell (1971) conducted a study in Hong Kong covering one of the most highly crowded communities in the world. He measured the exact size of each family's living space to compute inside density. He found no appreciable relationship between density and pathology. Booth and Welch (1974) also obtained similar findings.

In brief, the available studies reveal inconsistent findings. In most of the these studies tie inferences have been based on group data and in such cases individual factors have been inevitably ignored (Jain, 1985). One cannot eliminate the possibility that crowding may have serious effects on some people's mental health but not on others.

STUDIES OF CROWDING IN INDIA: In addition to the studies reported in this review, a few studies by psychologists have been carried out on Indian samples, a mention of which seems relevant.

In Allahabad, Nagar (1985) investigated the effects of high-low noise on performance on complex anagram and memory tasks. He found negative effects of noise as well as of density on complex task performance and affective feelings. In the second experiment he used a factorial design for manipulating density, noise, sex, and the experience of crowding. The results confirmed the findings of his first experiment and showed that subjects with greater experience of crowding performed better on comprehension of story task and complex anagram problems and exhibited more positive feelings as compared to subjects with less experience of crowding. Females performed better on the comprehension task and males on the complex anagram task. On the whole, no significant difference was obtained between males and females.

In a field survey, Nagar (1985) noted that respondents residing in high density experience greater crowding, perceive the interpersonal climate as less supportive and exhibit more adjustment problems. These findings have been interpreted in the light of the arousal model (Broadbent, 1971). Looking at these findings it can be suggested that the effects of crowding in India are similar to those reported in Western countries. Similar findings have also been reported by Anand (1983) who found adverse effects of high density on the quality of life, perceived control, health, feelings and personal space. The conclusion, however, remains to be checked across other situations.

In a survey of Varanasi city, Tripathi (1986) reported adverse effects of high density on feelings. The young and adult males from high density areas reported greater amount of stress than females. However, females in the older age group reported greater stress than males. Residents of high density were found to suffer from high anxiety.

The younger male subjects from high density localities were found to be poorly adjusted in their social environment. Greater frequency of neurotic tendency was also observed in high density rather than in low density areas. Tripathi (1986) concluded that the variables of adjustment, anxiety, and neuroticism were consistently related in the expected direction and inter-correlations became stronger with advancing age. In addition to the work done by psychologists some surveys of the responses to high density conditions have been conducted by Indian demographers, geographers, and sociologists. Kulkarni (1984) surveyed Ahmedabad city and found that the densely populated walled city experiences a high incidence of crime. Black marketing of cinema tickets and gambling are frequent crimes of the high density area. The walled city, being the core of the city for commercial, administrative, religious and cultural activities, is the scene of intense interaction often resulting in social conflicts and tensions. These findings may be generalised to other big cities—with a caution that several confounding variables may be operating simultaneously. For example, heterogeneity of population, level of industrialisation and type of short-term visitors may vary from one city to another and these factors are likely to moderate the effects of high density.

HIGH DENSITY AS A STRESSOR: The available empirical evidence relating high density to the feeling of crowding has revealed many negative consequences for human behaviour. Although these findings are not consistent, they do have theoretical and practical implications. If one looks at these findings in the larger context of environmental psychology, it becomes clear that high density and the feeling of crowding may be viewed as a stress component and an affective consequence, respectively. Noise, temperature, pollution and other man-made aspects of the environment, increasing size, and density of population constitute the components of an environmental stress complex. Within this framework high density is considered as a stressor and a noxious aspect of the environment. Recent research on environmental stress emphasises an understanding of those aspects of the environment which have the potential to produce aversive responses and the mechanisms underlying the evaluation of these aspects as sources of stress.

Credit goes to a biologist Hans Selye (1976, see Canter and Griffiths, 1982, p. 88) who introduced the concept of stress as a situation which is threatening to an organism and to which the organism reacts either to alter the situation or to withdraw himself from it. In a number of stages adaptation to the stressful situation takes place which has been termed as the General Adaptation Syndrome (GAS). The term stress is now extended from its biological flavour to its psychological texture. Perhaps it is the simultaneity of physiological and psychological reactions which characterise the stress condition.

In current usage the term stress is characterised in terms of psychological circumstances which produce aversive reactions to unfavourable physical conditions. Lazarus and Cohen (1977) have criticised the traditional approach to stress which emphasised only the possible external causes of stress. According to these authors it is on the basis of somatic, behavioural, and subjective responses that the stressing situation should be inferred. From this viewpoint the same situation might be stressing to some and not to others. Baum, Singer and Baum (1981) suggested that the threat which is considered as an attack on one's well being leads to the feeling of stress.

The inconsistent density-behaviour relationship when considered in the context of the modern concept of stress does not seem incoherent as a lot of subjectivity on the part of persons in high density determine the responses to crowding. The sources of subjective variations are many including the early experiences in high dense living, social and cultural norms, socio-economic status, sex, and availability of resources. Kirmayer (1978) in a review has attributed the diversity of results in research on crowding to cultural differences and socio-economic distribution. Similar findings have been obtained by Hawang (1979) who noted a greater degree of stress in crowding among low SES subjects. Altman and Chemers (1980) reported studies from various cultural groups and concluded that cross-cultural variations are evident in responses to crowding conditions.

In addition to the psychological determinants and effects of crowding physiological indicators of stress such as blood pressure, palmer sweat, illness complaints, suicides and mortality are also reported (D'Arti, Fitzgerald, Kasl and Ostfeld, 1981). These measures provide additional validity to the concept of crowding as stress.

Conceptualisation of crowding as an environmental stress has linked the analysis of crowding phenomenon to the dimension of perceived control, which plays a central role in integrating the diverse findings and their explanations in this field. As Stokols (1978b) has stated, 'The dimension of "perceived control" over the environment has become a central unifying concept in contemporary formulations of spatial behaviour' (p. 270).

In recent years considerable attention has been paid by researchers towards uncovering the consequences of crowding as an environmental stressor. As Cohen (1980) has argued that the physical characteristics of a potential environmental stressor are generally less important determinants than the psychological properties of the overall situation. The cognitive analysis of stressful episodes by Lazarus and Folkman (1984) indicates that for a situation to be deemed threatening the stimulus must be evaluated as harmful. According to them 'psychological stress has a particular relationship between the person and the environment that is appraised by the person as taxing or exceeding his or her resources and endangering his or her well being' (Lazarus and Folkman, 1984, p. 19). The process of threat appraisal is presumed to depend on the psychological structure of the individual and the cognitive features of the encountered stimulus situation. The desire for privacy has been proposed as an important determinant of stress reactions to density (Altman and Chemers, 1980). It is viewed as the freedom to decide about the social activity in which one participates.

Recent analysis of crowding has indicated that the feeling of control over one's environment mediated the effects of density-stress on behaviour and health. Seligman (1975) has argued that continual exposure to events, one can do nothing about, frequently results in a psychological state of helplessness. This state of helplessness includes a lessening of one's motivation to initiate new responses. Extreme effects of helplessness include fear, anxiety, depression, disease, and even death. However, it is the perception that one lacks control over an important outcome, not the physical stress itself, that produces stress related reactions.

The role of cognitive control in determining reactions to crowding has been analysed by a number of investigators. Provision of control reduces crowding deficits in performance and behavioural effects (Rodin and Baum, 1978; Schmidt and Keating, 1979). Also, there is evidence that the effects of residential density are mediated by the perception of control (Baum and Valins, 1977). The extremely poor and uneducated individuals and those living in institutions (susceptible population) when exposed to high levels of uncontrollable density show crowding effects which reinforce the feelings of powerlessness and helplessness. Rodin (1976) observed that the children living in high density settings expressed greater helplessness than their counterparts in low density settings. Studies of dormitories (Baum and Valins, 1979; Baum, Aiello and Calesnick, 1978) have also yielded similar results. The role of control, however, is probably more complex. According to Averill (1973), the stress reducing properties of personal control depend upon the meaning of the control response for the individual. Perceived crowding occurs only when a non-specific state of arousal is attributed to excessively close interpersonal proximity (Worchel, Brown and Webb, 1983). Combining control and attribution perspectives, Baron and Rodin (1978) have argued that density may not be experienced as uncontrollable unless the other people present are perceptually salient and unless blame for restricting one's freedom is attributed to their presence rather than to other factors in the situation (Schmidt and Keating, 1979). Both social and personal factors determine the perception of crowding (Stokols, Rall, Pinner and Schopler, 1978).

Recently, Ruback and Carr (1984) conducted a study in a prison for women. One of their hypotheses was that individuals who perceive greater control over their environment would feel less crowded than their counterparts who perceive less degree of control. The results showed that persons with greater perceived control expressed greater liking to their rooms as compared to those with low degree of perceived control and stress. In a number of Indian studies the fact that self perception and perception of the environment depend on the socio-economic status in which a person is immersed is brought out clearly (e.g., Jain and Surajmal, 1983; Misra and Shukla, 1986; Sinha, 1977).

In the light of the above discussion it seems reasonable to reiterate the importance of perception of high density situations and cognitive control in crowding research. Since the perception of environment and control is largely determined by the socio-cultural context and the individual's needs and desires we need a careful analysis of the impact of high density with reference to social conditions and personal characteristics (Jain and Misra, 1986). Investigators are now making an attempt to conceptualise crowding by obtaining descriptions of individual experiences of crowding and preparing taxonomic structures. These attempts have revealed the importance of experiences as a transactional process involving multiplicative interactions between an individual and his socio-physical situation (Van Staden, 1984). Cognitive process variables need to be identified for a better understanding of antecedents, moderators, and consequences of crowding.

THE PRESENT WORK: The findings of some empirical studies on crowding in the Indian setting have been discussed in the following pages. The Indian model pattern of physical-social environment can be characterised by high population density and scarcity of resources. Brown (1979) perceived this situation as a 'double edged sword' which increases demands and reduces the supply. Both high population density and scarcity of resources are viewed as stressors increasing excessive competition and influencing a variety of behavioural phenomena such as motivation, perception, affective state, interpersonal relation, desire for more personal space, and mental health. This author has investigated the effects of crowding on behaviour in both field and experimental studies. An attempt has also been made to test certain theoretical predictions related to personal space, competition tolerance and attribution. A relatively less investigated aspect of crowding has also been touched upon, i.e., crowding in rural versus urban residential settings. Finally, an attempt has been made to provide a conceptual model to explain the effects of crowding.

The studies reported in the volume are based on the assumption that the effects of high density under scarce resource conditions are much more severe because of the intense competition for the fulfilment of basic needs. Competition tolerance was viewed as an intervening condition between density and its motivational consequences. To determine the role of situational variables, the first study was undertaken in urban, semi-urban, and rural high-low dense areas. In addition, the role of education and heterogeneity on competition tolerance, need hierarchy and need intensity were also examined. The second study explored the feeling of crowding and social behaviour in relation to inside as well as outside density. The third study investigated the degree of interpersonal attraction, liking for neighbours and expected helping behaviour in low and middle socio-economic classes under high-low density living conditions. The fourth study examined the problem of mental health in relation to high-low density and the feeling of crowding. The fifth and final study experimentally examined the effects of scarcity of resources and density on the feeling of crowding and desired personal space.

— 2 —

Effects of
Crowding on
Motivation

The nature of human beings' interaction with the environment partly depends upon population characteristics, the nature of socio-cultural needs, and the distribution of available resources in society. An affluent society affords to provide better facilities to its members through which they are able to overcome the adversities of the environment. On the other hand, economically poor countries with their limited resources are handicapped in facing an aversive environment effectively. In the present age particularly the people of countries following the Western model of development seem to be competing for the available resources. The competition becomes increasingly intense if the number of competitors are more. Hence, competitiveness seems to be linked with population growth.

As population grows in size, density and heterogeneity also grow and individuals face increasingly greater and bitter competition (Fox, 1975). They have to compete with others even in meeting their basic needs such as shelter, food, transportation, and recreation. In large cities waiting in queues for basic essentials is a very common experience. Studies on competition were conducted in laboratory situations and it would not be out of place to mention a few of them in this context. Scott and Cherrington (1974) examined the effect of competitive, cooperative, and individualistic reinforcement contingencies. In this study subjects in the competitive group produced more, reported higher levels of arousal, and less interpersonal attraction as compared to subjects in cooperative or individualistic contingency groups. Those who were rewarded in various conditions reported higher levels of interpersonal and task attractiveness. Berlyne (1967) and Fowler (1970) found that individuals exposed to a competitive social situation reported greater levels of arousal, receptor orientation, negative behaviour of coactors and higher level of performance.

Pettigrew (1967) commented that in a competitive society the satisfaction of differentiating reward and the feeling of competitive success are greater than compensation for the interpersonal loss. In contrast to Pettigrew's (1967) dual hypothesis is Horney's (1939) view which suggests that competition is a major cause of interpersonal conflict. The results of some studies (Deutsch, 1953) seem to confirm this assertion. Rabbie, Benoist, Oosterbaan and Visser (1974) found that competitive groups were more hostile and had more negative attitude towards other groups as compared to cooperative groups. On the other hand, competition has also been found to improve interpersonal relations (Myers, 1962). Gormly, Gormly and Johnson (1971) suggested that disagreements are more salient than agreements in consideration of attitudes towards others. If agreements and disagreements have different reinforcing values in influencing attraction, then the Byrne-Clore's (1970) reinforcement paradigm would suggest that a large number of topics (and hence a greater number of disagreements within the proportion of agreements) would yield lower attraction.

These studies suggest the possible influence of competition on social behaviour. Since population growth accelerates competition, interpersonal behaviour is bound to be affected. Another consequence of overpopulation on individuals is the feeling of insecurity and loss of identity due to dissatisfaction of social needs. Again, there may be persons whose social needs are more intense than others (Rosen, 1956). Individuals may differ not only in terms of intensity of their social needs but also in terms of hierarchy of needs (Maslow, 1962).

In case of success one competes for higher goals. Those who fail to compete with others in achieving their goals, have no other choice than to substitute their goals or to change their need patterns. Motivational theories (Maslow, 1962; Murray, 1962) support this contention that need pattern changes according to the experience and attainments of various goals.

Competition Tolerance

Competition has two connotations. First, it is an intervening motivational variable 'self chosen motive to excel', and second, it is a condition of the society which is thrust upon the individual. An individual's behaviour will be a product of the interaction of both these aspects of competition. Social, psychological, anthropological, and sociological literature is replete with illustrations of the impact of situational variables on personality. Mead (1961) has reported many studies on competition which show that there are cultural and social differences in the amount of competitiveness among individuals. They are, thus, to a large extent responsible for the observed individual differences in competitiveness.

Competition tolerance can be perceived as the capacity of an individual to face competitive situations. It refers to the capacity of an individual to face competition directly; without using defence mechanisms and without withdrawing from the situations encountered. Thus, it is a motivational characteristic which may be a consequence of one's life experiences. Once this tolerance develops it may also affect the behavioural pattern of the person.

Rosen (1956) has accepted competition feeling as one of the components of need achievement. An individual with high need achievement prefers a competitive situation where he can perform according to the standards of excellence (McClelland, Atkinson, Clark and Lowell, 1953). Even in the absence of a competitive situation one may set one's own standards of excellence and persistently strive to attain them. The present concept is different from the concept of need achievement in as much as it connotes the impact of persistent social situation on the individual. It is not like the high need achievement which sustains behaviour and is manifested in any work the individual may engage in. Competition tolerance is supposedly manifested in competitive situations and may sustain behaviours in similar situations. Repetitive exposure to competitive situations are supposed to increase competition tolerance.

Need Hierarchy Pattern

A need is a hypothetical state presumed to energise and sustain behaviour till goal attainment. There are persons whose social needs are more intense than others (Atkinson, 1958). Individuals differ not only in terms of the intensity of social needs but also in terms of the pattern or hierarchy of needs. Population growth may produce conditions of more intense competition for survival and for the fulfilment of social needs. Density and heterogeneity of population may increase the intensity of various needs (Freedman, 1975). The hierarchy of human needs is not permanently established but is constantly subject to change according to social pressures. Murray (1938) has defined some important needs as follows:

DOMINANCE: The dominance need is manifested by a desire to control the sentiments, behaviour, and ideas of others. The general actions are to influence, to persuade, to regulate, to judge, and to make laws.

DEFERENCE: This need is characterised by feelings and emotions of respect, admiration, wonder and reverence. The main traits and attitudes are respect, admiration, worship and general actions to accept the leadership of a more experienced person.

AUTONOMY: This need controls those who wish neither to lead nor to be led; those who want to go on their own way uninfluenced by others. It is also characterised by the desire to avoid or quit activities prescribed by dominating authorities, to be independent, and free to act according to impulses and to defy conventions.

AGGRESSION: There are three types of aggression included in this category:

(a) *Emotional and Verbal.* This type of aggression is manifested in hate (whether or not the feeling is expressed in words), anger, verbal quarrel, abuses, criticisms, reproval, blame, ridicule and in arousing aggression against another person by public criticism.

(b) *Physical and Social.* It is expressed in fighting or killing in self defence or in defence of a loved object, avenging an unprovoked insult, fighting for a good cause, punishing an offender, and catching a criminal or an enemy.

(c) *Physical and Asocial.* This is manifested in a hold up, an attack, an attempt to injure, to initiate a fight without due cause. and to fight against legally constituted authorities.

ABASEMENT: Directly opposed to aggression is abasement need. To submit to coercion or restraint in order to avoid blame or punishment or pain or death. To suffer a disagreeable press (insult, injury, defeat) without opposition, to confess, to apologise, promise to do better, and to admit inferiority, a mistake or wrong doing. The general actions are to adopt a passive, meek and humble attitude. to stand aside, to take a back seat and let others push by having the best.

ACHIEVEMENT: Achievement may accompany other needs. It is a desire or a tendency to do things as rapidly or as well as possible. The person has a desire to accomplish something difficult. To master, manipulate or organise physical objects, human beings or ideas; to overcome obstacles; and attain a high standard so as to excel. The general actions are to make intense, prolonged and repeated efforts, to accomplish something difficult, to enjoy competition.

AFFILIATION: It represents a positive tropism for people. The person enjoys the cooperative company of others, or tries to please and win the affection of others, and wants to remain loyal to a friend. The main emotions are trust, goodwill, affection and love.

SUCCORANCE: Succorance is the tendency to cry, or to ask for nourishment, love, protection or aid, the person wants to be nursed and supported, surrounded and protected.

NURTURANCE: This is characterised by sympathy in action. Individuals with nurturance need want to be kind and considerate to others, to encourage, aid, protect, defend or rescue an object. They are liberal with energy and money when their compassion is aroused.

ORDER: This need order describes behavioural trends that are directed towards the organisation of the immediate environment, cleanliness and care of the body, arrangement of positions, placing things in their proper place, orderliness of drawers, desk, books, etc.

Intensity of any of the needs reflects the concern of the individual with related goal objects. Similarly the hierarchy of needs reflects the individual's relative priority of different needs. Need intensity and hierarchy are not necessarily related, as many a times our preferences may not be determined by our actual necessities but by their momentary significance decided by situational potentialities and the individual's immediate concern. Thus situational as well as the individual's characteristic factors seem to jointly influence need intensity and hierarchy. In the present context competition tolerance is an individual related factor and density is a situational factor.

In a developing country like India the scarcity of resources can be marked in almost every field, such as education, medicine, employment, agriculture, housing and industries. Of the various causes of scarcity, such as unequal distribution and dominance of a few people over the available resources, increasing population is one of the factors of scarcity. Every impressive index of growth in our country has failed to yield optimum results because of the increasing number of people. The magnitude of scarcity of resources can also be estimated by the wide socio-economic disparities among the people in urban as well as rural areas. Official records from various sources show that 40 to 50 per cent of our population is below the poverty line. In such a situation intense competition and change in the need pattern seems to be one of the probable effects of high density. With this assumption it was expected that people of high-low density areas would differ in terms of competition tolerance and need pattern. More specifically, it was hypothesised that the residents of high density areas would show greater competition tolerance than the residents of low density areas.

The argument that high density leads to a situation of high competition because of limited resources is based on the fact that the available space for a person in a high density situation is lesser than that in a low density situation. Space has also been perceived as a resource in the ecological model of crowding (Wicker and Kirmeyer, 1977). Thus high density as a limited resource condition can be thought of as conducive to high competition.

Effects of scarce resources have been amply documented in the research on dependency and collectivism in India. For example, J.B.P.Sinha (1968) has observed that under limited resource conditions output was reduced, subjects showed less liking for the group and even gave negative evaluations of self. These findings can be generalised to high density conditions. Scarcity of resources compels individuals to struggle for power so that they can monopolise the resources (J.B.P. Sinha, 1985). Struggle for power and/or for monopolisation of available resources initiates competition particularly when the number of competitors are increasing. Increasing population in its manifestation of high density and heterogeneity constantly persuade individuals to compete. Those who develop high competition tolerance are supposed to participate in competition and those who do not are supposed to withdraw themselves.

Against this background a survey study was designed to answer the following research questions.

1. In what ways are population density, heterogeneity and urban-rural settings related to competition tolerance?
2. Whether need pattern can be regarded as a function of population characteristics and competition tolerance? In other words, whether need patterns are different in different sizes of population, in heterogeneous and homogeneous populations, and in high and low population densities?
3. Whether there is any change in the need intensities with variations in population density, heterogeneity and size of population?

Method

Participants

Two groups consisting of 195 males drawn from high and low dense areas selected from urban, semi-urban and rural residential settings participated in the study. These groups were largely matched in terms of age, occupation, socio-economic status (SES), place of origin, and family size. However, groups from different areas could not be matched because of differential social composition of the population of urban, semi-urban and rural areas. In each of these areas houses were randomly selected and from each selected household one adult male member was included in the sample. The total sample comprised of 390 participants. The description of the areas selected for study is given below and the details of the sample are given in Table 1.

Table 1. Composition of Different Groups

Variables	Urban		Semi-Urban		Rural	
	HD	LD	HD	LD	HD	LD
OCCUPATION						
Service	74	70	17	0	4	5
Business	8	10	21	1	20	15
Agriculture	0	2	4	49	15	20
Others	13	13	8	0	11	10
FAMILY SIZE						
1 to 4 members	26	26	7	13	7	5
5 and above	69	69	43	37	43	45
AGE						
20 to 30 years	64	66	32	37	23	26
31 to 40 years	16	12	14	13	11	18
41 years and above	15	17	4	0	16	6
Total	95	95	50	50	50	50

HD = High Density
LD = Low Density

Brief Descriptions of the Areas Selected for Study

JAIPUR: The capital of Rajasthan state, Jaipur is known as the Pink City because of its historical grandeur and splendid colourful architecture. The old, walled part of the city was planned by the famous architect Vidyadhar. Originally the various residential wards of the city were inhabited on the basis of caste, so that each ward was inhabited by a particular caste group. Later developments in residential areas outside as well as inside the walled city have transformed Jaipur into a metropolitan town. In spite of this the various wards of the walled city have maintained their historical texture to a great extent. The walled city is densely populated while the outskirt colonies are relatively less dense. On the basis of census records the high and low population areas were identified. In the 1971 Census, the total city had been divided into 38 census wards. Ward No. 11 was selected representing a low density area and Ward No. 32 represented a high density area.

CHAKSU: A semi-urban town situated about 40 kms south east of Jaipur on the National highway. It is accessible by bus as well as by train. This town covers about 2 sq kms area. According to the 1971 census the population of the area was about 10,411 persons living in 1970 houses. About three-fourths of the houses are made of stone and the remaining are huts. The main caste groups living in this town apart from Muslims and Jains are Jats, Gujars, Malis, Meenas, Raigers and Chamars. Most of the people living here are workers (daily wages) and a few of them are businessmen. The land is quite fertile and there are good water sources. Therefore, a fairly large number of individuals are also engaged in farming. Most of the farmers are Muslims. The main government departments and social service agencies are the dispensary, the municipality, a higher secondary school, the panchayat samiti, the public works department, a police station, the Nagar Congress Committee, the Krishi Upaj Mandi, etc. The whole town is divided into seven wards. Some of the wards in the interior are thickly populated while the rest of them are sparsely populated.

In the present study data were collected from the most thickly populated as well as the most sparsely populated wards.

BADHAL: Badhal is a big village in Jaipur district. Its population is about 4,918 and the houses number about 500. The village covers about one sq km area. About 80 per cent of the houses are small and made of stone, and the remaining 20 per cent are huts. The residents of Badhal speak the local language as well as Hindi. There is a higher secondary school, a dispensary and a good market in the village. The dominant caste here is Bania, other castes include Dhobi, Jats, Rajputs, Chamars, etc. Business is the dominating profession of this area.

For the purpose of the present study data from two different wards have been collected. One ward was thickly populated and the other was sparsely populated. The total population and density of the areas are given below:

Area per Square Kilometre and Population According to 1961, 1971, 1981 Census Reports

Place	Area (per sq. km.)	Density of Population per sq. km.	Population
Jaipur	64.75 (1961)	2986	403444
	206.06 (1971)		615258
	(1981)		977165
Chaksu	40.61 (1961)	256	8063
	40.62 (1971)		10411
	(1981)		14213
Badhal	16.50 (1961)	273	3870
	28.00 (1971)		4918

Note: The study was conducted at the time when the 1981 Census was not available.

Measures

COMPETITION TOLERANCE: Considering the earlier mentioned concept, a psychometric measure of competition tolerance was developed by the author (Jain, 1976) as a part of the study. The items of the tests were framed on the basis of interviews of individuals drawn from various strata who were asked to describe some situations where they experienced acute competition. Each of the framed items described one competitive situation. Four answer categories, describing the possible reactions to the stated situation, were available along with each item. In each case the first answer category described maximum participation, the second category described low participation, the third category represented no-participation and the last category showed complete withdrawal. In addition, the participants were allowed to mention any other alternative they thought was true for them. Separate forms of the test were prepared for urban and rural samples. Items included in the urban form described competitive situations related to urban areas and the rural form described rural situations.

Test-retest reliabilities for urban and rural samples were estimated at .76 and .72, respectively. Similarly split-half reliabilities for the two groups were estimated at .65 and .62, respectively. The measure was experimentally validated.

One illustrative item from the urban form of competition tolerance test is in order.

'Suppose you have decided to start a small scale industry in your town. Before you could implement your plan, you come to know that someone else has already started a similar industry. Now what would you like to do?

(a) Would you still start the same industry on a larger scale.
(b) Would you start the industry according to your original plan.
(c) Would you plan some other new industry.
(d) Would you give up the idea of industry.'

NEED HIERARCHY LADDER: To ascertain the need hierarchy patterns of the participants all the ten needs were described separately in the form of simple and short sentences. These sentences along with the figure of a ladder with ten steps were presented to the participants. They were requested to place the most relevant sentence at the top of the ladder and the least relevant at the bottom. To do this the participants were asked to read/listen to all the sentences and then to select the one that was most relevant for him and place it at the top of the ladder. After that he was further requested to read/listen to the rest of the items and select one to place on the second step of the ladder. This procedure was repeated until all the items were placed on the ladder by the participant. The ladder technique has been profitably used in studies of motivation (Misra and Tripathi, 1978; Sinha, 1969). For the present purpose this technique was used to assess the need hierarchy pattern of the subjects for it provides a situation where subjects can make a simultaneous comparison between different needs. The test-retest reliability of the test was .83.

NEED QUESTIONNAIRE: To measure the intensity of various needs a questionnaire was adopted in Hindi based on the Edwards (1954) Personal Preference Schedule (EPPS). The EPPS contains items related to various needs. But for the present study ten needs were selected which were suggested by judges as relevant to the Indian society. These needs are—achievement, deference, order, autonomy, nurturance, abasement, succorance, affiliation, dominance, and aggression. Five items related to each of the ten needs were translated into Hindi and modified to suit the present requirements. All the fifty items were randomly arranged. The main feature of this measure is that every need is placed against each other and, therefore, the participant is able to imagine the comparative intensity of each need. The test-retest reliability of this measure was estimated at .84.

Procedure

In urban areas each participant was individually contacted and the measures were administered in two sessions. In semi-urban and rural areas these measures were largely used as interview schedules. The investigators read aloud each item and then clarified in the local dialect and recorded the responses. The items of the competition tolerance test described familiar situations and subjects were requested to imagine themselves facing the described situation. Thus every possible care was taken to ensure that the participants were following the instructions. The ladder test and need questionnaire were also administered individually.

Results

Competition Tolerance

The distribution of competition tolerance scores is given in Figure 1. Table 2 reveals that the residents from high density areas in urban and rural areas evinced greater competition tolerance than their low density counterparts. However, the trend in semi-urban areas was in the opposite direction where greater competition tolerance was observed in low density areas. The explanation for this trend is given in a later section of this chapter.

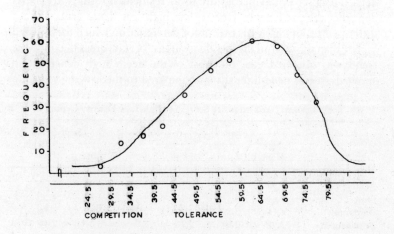

FIG. 1   DISTRIBUTION OF SCORES

Table 2. Mean Scores of Competition Tolerance for High-Low Density Groups

Area	Density	Mean	Mean Difference	Rp Values
Urban	High	71.36	2.88	2.873*
Urban	Low	68.48		
Rural	High	58.40	18.32	3.123*
Rural	Low	40.08		
Semi-Urban	High	51.14	4.32	2.873*
Semi-Urban	Low	55.46		

*p < .5

Need Intensity

Table 3 shows the differences in intensity of needs in high-low dense areas separately across the three residential settings. It is evident that the participants from urban high-low dense areas did not differ in intensity of needs except for deference on which they scored higher than those from the low dense areas. In rural areas the opposite trend was obtained, i.e., on most of the needs high dense group showed greater need intensity as compared to the low dense group

Table 3. Mean Need Intensity Scores of High-Low Density Groups

Needs	Urban		Rural		Semi-Urban	
	High	Low	High	Low	High	Low
Achievement	3.98	3.82	2.78	2.20	3.80	3.62
Order	4.54	4.38	3.16[b]	2.72[b]	4.82[j]	4.00[j]
Autonomy	4.14	3.82	2.96[c]	2.28[c]	3.66	3.44
Dominance	2.98	2.94	2.78[d]	2.06[d]	3.04[k]	2.44[k]
Aggression	1.56	1.56	2.70[e]	2.22[e]	1.30	1.02
Deference	3.88[a]	3.44[a]	2.96[f]	1.92[f]	3.66	3.46
Abasement	3.86	3.84	3.00[g]	2.32[g]	3.60	3.50
Nurturance	4.50	4.34	3.20[h]	2.58[h]	4.70[t]	4.30[t]
Succorance	3.08	2.68	2.64	2.56	4.26	3.16
Affiliation	4.30	4.26	2.88[i]	2.16[i]	4.08	3.74

Note: Means with common script differ significantly in terms of Rp values. $p < .05$ other means do not differ significantly.

except for achievement and succorance needs. In semi-urban areas the high dense group showed greater intensity of *n* order, *n* dominance, and *n* nurturance as compared to the low dense group. The two groups did not differ significantly in relation to the other needs. These trends are graphically depicted in Figures 3 to 5.

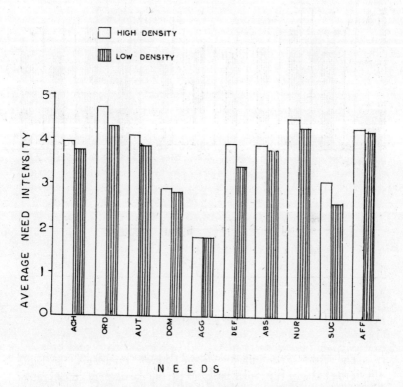

FIG. 3   NEED   INTENSITY   URBAN GROUPS

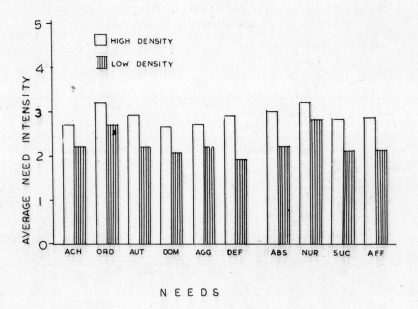

N E E D S

FIG. 4   NEED INTENSITY   RURAL GROUPS

Need Pattern

The responses obtained using the Ladder Test are given in Table 4. On the basis of the ranks assigned by the participants mean ranks for each group on each need were obtained. The ranks revealed that the high-low dense groups in urban areas did not differ in their need patterns. However, in rural areas the high dense group preferred *n* dominance to a greater degree as compared to the other needs whereas the low dense group preferred *n* abasement. In the semi-urban area the two groups preferred similar needs on the ladder.

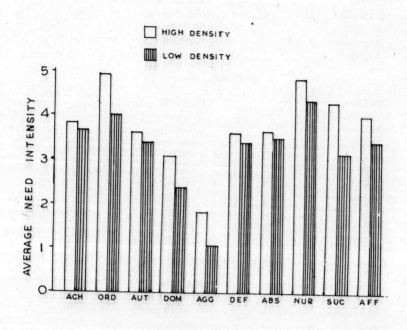

FIG. 5   NEED INTENSITY   SEMI-URBAN GROUPS

Table 4. Rank Order of Need Patterns in Different Groups

URBAN AREA

Low Dense
Order
Autonomy
Achievement
Nurturance
Affiliation

High Dense
Order
Autonomy
Achievement
Nurturance
Affiliation

(Contd.)

Low Dense	High Dense
Deference	Deference
Succorance	Succorance
Dominance	Dominance
Abasement	Abasement
Aggression	Aggression

RURAL AREA

Low Dense	High Dense
Abasement	Dominance
Nurturance	Abasement
Dominance	Affiliation
Affiliation	Nurturance
Succorance	Succorance
Order	Order
Autonomy	Autonomy
Aggression	Achievement
Deference	Aggression
Achievement	Deference

SEMI-URBAN AREA

Low Dense	High Dense
Dominance	Aggression
Achievement	Nurturance
Aggression	Dominance
Abasement	Abasement
Nurturance	Affiliation
Order	Order
Deference	Deference
Affiliation	Autonomy
Succorance	Succorance
Autonomy	Achievement

Competition Tolerance and Need Intensity

To determine the relationship between competition tolerance and need intensity the data were pooled to form extreme groups. The high (above Q_3) and low (up to Q_1) competition tolerant groups, from the urban high dense samples, were identified. Table 5 indicates greater intensity of all the needs, with the exception of n aggression and n succorance in case of the high density group (see Figure 2).

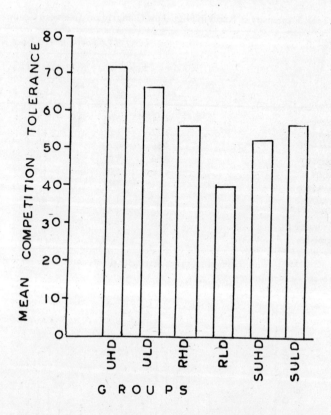

FIG. 2   COMPETITION   TOLERANCE

Competition Tolerance and Need Pattern

The means obtained for each need on the Ladder Test were
ranked for high and low competition tolerant groups. The low score
represents a higher preference on the Ladder Test. The results (Table
6) indicated that n order and n nurturance were assigned the highest
rank by the high and low competitive tolerant groups. (see Figure 6).

Table 5. Intensity of Needs in High-Low Competition Tolerance Groups

| Needs | Level of Competition Tolerance | | | |
| | High | | Low | |
	Mean	SD	Mean	SD
Achievement	4.04	0.93	2.52	1.04
Deference	3.32	1.21	2.16	0.94
Order	4.56	0.70	3.04	0.97
Autonomy	3.56	1.03	2.60	1.00
Affiliation	4.04	1.01	2.44	1.20
Succorance	3.04[a]	1.45	2.68[a]	1.02
Dominance	2.93	1.50	2.28	1.02
Abasement	3.76	1.33	2.60	1.03
Nurturance	4.08	0.99	3.20	0.95
Aggression	1.88[b]	1.33	2.28[b]	1.04

Means with common scripts do not differ significantly, other mean differences are significant, $*p < .01$

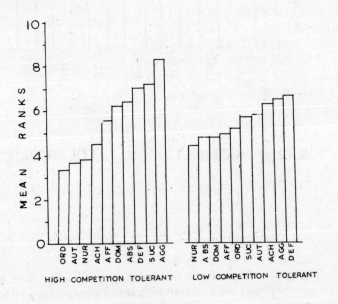

FIG. 6   NEED HIERARCHY

**Table 6. Rank Order of Need Pattern of
High and Low Competition Tolerance Groups**

High Competition Tolerance			Low Competition Tolerance		
Needs	M	Rank	Needs	M	Rank
Order	3.30	1	Nurturance	4.36	1
Autonomy	3.58	2	Abasement	4.75	2.5
Nurturance	3.77	3	Dominance	4.75	2.5
Achievement	4.45	4	Affiliation	4.96	4
Affiliation	5.53	5	Order	5.17	5
Dominance	6.26	6	Succorance	5.72	6
Abasement	6.46	7	Autonomy	5.75	7
Deference	7.03	8	Achievement	6.29	8
Succorance	7.18	9	Aggression	6.52	9
Aggression	8.36	10	Deference	6.58	10

Homogeneity-Heterogeneity and Competition Tolerance

The urban samples were categorised as homogeneous and heterogeneous on the basis of occupation and income. The homogeneous group comprised of persons in government and semi-government jobs and the heterogeneous group included persons engaged in diverse jobs and with varied incomes. The two groups were similar on competition tolerance, the mean scores were 66.21 and 64.90 for homogeneous and heterogeneous groups, respectively. Their need pattern was almost similar as shown in Table 7.

Education, Competition Tolerance and Need Intensity

Another classification of the urban sample was made on the basis of level of education. The low education group had received high school or less education and the high education group had formal education up to the graduate or post-graduate level. The two groups were compared for competition tolerance and need intensity. Table 8 shows that highly educated participants showed greater competition tolerance than participants whose level of education was low. In addition, highly educated participants showed less intensity of n succorance.

Table 7. Rank for Needs in Homogeneous and Heterogeneous Groups

Homogeneous Group		Heterogeneous Group	
Needs	Rank Mean	Needs	Rank Mean
Autonomy	2.00	Order	1.90
Order	2.65	Autonomy	3.25
Achievement	3.85	Nurturance	4.85
Nurturance	4.10	Affiliation	5.20
Dominance	6.20	Achievement	5.30
Affiliation	6.50	Deference	5.50
Abasement	7.20	Succorance ·	5.90
Succorance	7.50	Dominance	8.50
Deference	7.70	Abasement	8.50
Aggression	7.80	Aggression	8.85

r between need pattern of homogeneous and heterogeneous group = .79, $p < .01$

n nurturance, n affiliation and n aggression. The two groups did not differ significantly on other needs as shown in Table 8.

Table 8. Competition Tolerance and Need Intensity in High and Low Educated Groups

Measures	Level of Education		
	High	Low	t (93)
Competition Tolerance	64.50	61.50	2.27*
n Achievement	3.75	3.42	0.35
n Deference	3.32	3.55	1.43
n Order	4.25	4.08	1.06
n Autonomy	3.60	3.48	0.48
n Affiliation	4.02	3.46	3.5*
n Succorance	2.75	3.25	2.88*
n Dominance	2.73	2.85	0.8
n Abasement	3.55	3.50	0.29
n Nurturance	4.15	3.65	2.00*
n Aggression	1.60	2.06	2.46*

*$p < .05$

Discussion

Competition tolerance is regarded as an individual's capacity to cope with his environment. As an intervening psychological state its degree varies with variations in population density. High density situation leads to high competition which motivates the residents to compete more and more for fulfilling their needs. The experiences of such a situation are likely to develop high competition tolerance. The present study shows that urban people from densely populated areas manifested a higher degree of competition tolerance than urban people living in low dense areas. A similar pattern for competition tolerance was seen in the rural groups. Furthermore, high dense urban residents showed greater competition tolerance than high dense rural residents. Similar results have been obtained by Freedman et al (1971) in an experimental study which showed that boys competed more in crowded rooms. Thus repeated participation in competitive situations is likely to develop competition tolerance. A high density condition seems to be a condition for competition for scarce resources. If the resources are limited people cannot share them. Under constant competitive situations of high population density people hardly find the time to think about others. They compete for scarce facilities and gradually adapt themselves to such an environment. In other words, the individual develops competition tolerance as a way of adaptation. Adaptation to an overloaded (over populated) social environment may result in disregard for the needs of other people (Heimstra and McDonald, 1973). Milgram (1970) suggests that 'adaptation of urban dwellers leads to changes in cognitive processes i.e. inability to identify most of the people he sees daily, his screening of sensory stimuli and his selectivity in responding to human demands.'

The present study shows that adaptation to high density demands high competition tolerance. This finding is in line with the control model of crowding (Rodin, 1976). For increasing the degree of control over the environment one has to be motivated to compete with others. Furthermore, the high competition tolerance group showed greater preference for higher social needs and their need pattern (Figure 6) was different from that of the low competition tolerant group. It should be recalled that these needs were measured by a

modified EPPS which was designed to minimise the influence of
social attitudes and values in response to the statements (Freeman,
1965). These needs have been derived from the needs listed by Murray
(1938) and indicate the personality of the individual. Therefore, personality
characteristics associated with the degree of competition tolerance can
also be examined from the obtained profiles. Individuals with high competition tolerance prefer arrangement, organisation, balance, neatness,
tidiness and precision more than other things, as shown in their need
rankings, because success in competition depends on these factors.

Intensity of *n* order was highest in the high competition tolerance
group. However, the low competition tolerance group assigned the
highest rank to *n* nurturance, which shows their preference for sym-
pathising the helpless and weaker persons. The contrast between the
two groups is evident here. A person with low competition tolerance
seems to be helpful and considerate towards others and this characteristic may prevent him from being in a competitive situation. In contrast,
a person with high competition tolerance perfers orderliness so that he
may plan his actions to get things done properly in his interest. This is
also evident from the results obtained: need achievement is higher in
persons with high competition tolerance than in those with low competition tolerance. In a number of studies (e.g., Edward and Jacob, 1975;
McGuire and Thomas, 1975; Okum and Vesta, 1975; Shaw, 1971) competitive situations have been regarded as motivating situations. In this
sense high competition tolerant persons can be perceived as persons
with stronger motivation to plan their actions for high achievement.

Thus the present results show a clear relationship between population density and competition tolerance. However, the relationship
between population density and need pattern independent of competition tolerance is ambiguous. As has been reported, urban residents of high and low dense areas did not show any marked difference
in motivation. It seems that because of the influence of other factors
like urbanisation, rather than population density, residents of high
and low dense areas develop similar preferences. Unlike the variation
in competition tolerance amongst the residents of high and low dense
areas, need intensity and need pattern of urban people were more or
less similar. In the present context it seems that density affects competition tolerance which, in turn, affects need intensity and need pattern of persons. Even in the absence of the effects of urbanisation,
need intensity seems to be related to density. This is evident from the
results obtained from the rural population. The rural high dense

group showed higher intensity for all the needs with the exception of n achievement and n succorance. These results are in line with the expectations of this study. Nearly all the needs are more intense in high dense residents showing high competition tolerance. The results show that in urban areas density *per se* does not seem to influence the need pattern. In contrast, competition tolerance as an intervening variable is related to population density on the one hand and need hierarchy on the other.

Heterogeneity of population is a characteristic of urban population (Milgram, 1970). On this consideration the urban sample was categorised as homogeneous and heterogeneous. These groups, however, did not show a significant difference in competition tolerance. Residents of a city may view other persons whether of similar occupations or castes, as equally important candidates with whom they have to compete. The need for control over the environment motivates them to compete with everyone. In fact George Simmel (Quoted by Milgram, 1970) has pointed out that 'since urban dwellers come into contact with vast number of people each day, they conserve psychic energy by becoming acquainted with a far smaller proportion of people than their rural counterparts do'. Several other studies (e.g., EoYang, 1974; Griffitt and Veitch, 1971; Hutt and Vaizey, 1966; Loo, 1972; Proshansky, 1973) have shown reduced interpersonal relationships in overpopulated areas. Perhaps, it is a demand of the situation that involves more and more competition which tends to develop such interpersonal relationships in high dense areas. However, further study is required to test this hypothesis. Homogeneous and heterogeneous groups seem equally competitive, perhaps because of the demands of the social situation to possess more and more in the direction of enhancing control over situations.

In congruence with the findings, heterogeneous and homogeneous urban groups did not differ in the hierarchy of need pattern which clearly indicates somewhat similar need hierarchy across both the groups. In fact there was a high correlation (rho = .79) between the need patterns of the two groups. Here, it may be recalled that heterogeneous and homogeneous groups did not differ in competition tolerance. It has been shown that competition tolerance is related to need intensity and pattern, therefore, when the degree of competition tolerance is more or less equal in the two groups the need pattern of heterogeneous and homogeneous groups ought to be correlated.

Examining these results in the light of crowding effects, one can see a parallel between the results obtained in laboratory studies and in actual living conditions. Various studies on crowding (Mehrabian and Russell, 1974; Munroe and Munroe, 1972; Sommer, 1969) have repeatedly shown the negative influence of high population density on the individual's social and affective functioning. The present study has shown the development of competition tolerance as a result of high population density. To this extent, high density cannot be regarded as an adverse condition since the resulting motivation leads to personal growth. If, high degree of competition tolerance leads to the growth of higher needs (e.g., *n* order and *n* ach) it has to be viewed as a favourable effect. However, competition tolerance at some point may become so high that the individual's interpersonal relationships and consideration of others' needs may be disturbed. This possibility, if true, will be in agreement with crowding effects. But this has yet to be investigated.

The sample from the semi-urban population has shown a specific trend. The greater degree of competition tolerance in the low dense areas and the absence of clear-cut differences in the need patterns of high and low dense groups can be explained in terms of other differences between the two groups and the characteristics of the population of the area selected here. *Chaksu,* the semi-urban area in the study, is a small village and has only recently developed as a town because of large-scale migration from the city. In fact these migrants have outnumbered the original inhabitants of this place. The low dense area selected in this study was inhabited by these migrants and this may explain the underlying high competition tolerance in the low dense group. An in-depth study is warranted to assess the characteristics of migrants in the cities.

The concept of competition tolerance seems useful in explaining the psycho-ecological dynamics. The present findings have established that competition tolerance varies from one density to the other. Also, highly educated persons exhibited greater competition tolerance. The association of density and education with competition tolerance supports the contention that greater the experience and awareness of competitive situations more the competition tolerance.

In conclusion, the study has revealed a clear effect of density on competition tolerance of the residents from urban as well as rural areas. The intensity of needs seems to be influenced by density in the absence of urbanisation. However, density with urbanisation seems to influence competition tolerance but not the need hierarchy or intensity of needs.

— 3 —

Effect of
Population Density on
Social Behaviour

In the earlier study association of objective crowding with motivation was investigated and it was observed that competition tolerance moderates the effects of objective crowding. The measure of objective crowding was area density which is not a very precise measure of density. The present study is aimed at comparing the effects of outside and inside density on certain social behaviours and subjective aspects of crowding.

In recent research on crowding social interaction has been considered as a mediator between population density and social behaviour (Aiello and Baum, 1979; Sundstrom, 1975). Social behaviours such as laughing, non-verbal expression, aggression, affiliation, feelings of group cohesion, interpersonal relations, liking for strangers, and competition tolerance have been reported to be associated with population density (Baum and Davis, 1976; Bergman, 1971; Hutt and Vaizey, 1966; Jain, 1978; Stokols et al, 1973). These studies have generally shown that the subjective feeling of crowding and population density are not necessarily correlated. The distinction between crowding and population density suggests that density is a necessary but not a sufficient condition to produce crowding.

Outside — Inside Density and the Feeling of Crowding

High dense urban setting has been conceptualised as a condition of 'stimulus overload' (Milgram, 1970) which is supposed to create psychological stress associated with crowding. In view of the distinction between population density and crowding and the inconsistent results of some studies (Freedman et al, 1971; Griffitt and Veitch, 1971) it can be argued that all types of population density, even in urban areas, may not be associated with the feeling of crowding and negative social behaviour. Some researchers have found that it is associated with certain positive effects. On the basis of this possibility the present study was conducted to explore social behaviour in day-to-day living across high and low outside density and high and low inside density conditions.

Inside density refers to the number of inhabitants in a house in proportion to available space, while outside density is the total population of a given locality. It was hypothesised that high population density inside the house would be associated with negative feelings and negative social behaviours. A similar prediction was not made in the case of outside density because sufficient space inside the house may reduce the negative effects of outside density, if any. Thus the present study is aimed at exploring these aspects of day-to-day life which covary along with population density.

Method

Sample (Outside density)

On the basis of census records a high dense locality was identified in Jaipur town. Keeping in view the type of houses in the walled area of Jaipur and to control the family size by matching the high-low density groups, fifty houses were selected which could fulfill the following conditions: availability and willingness of an adult male member to participate in the study; the family should belong to the lower middle class; and the house should have two to three rooms to accommodate four to six family members. Keeping in view the matching variables, i.e., SES, age, and education, similar samples were drawn from a low density area. A hundred male adults participated in this study. Description of the areas selected is given below.

SHASTRI NAGAR: A new housing board colony situated outside the walled city on Jhotwara Road with a population of 70,811. In this colony houses are located on both sides of the road. Each house has an equal area and is surrounded by a wall. Every house has small open area in the front which is used as a small garden in almost every house. Each house has four rooms with large windows and ventilators. On the whole single families live in each house with only a few exceptions. Due to the distance between houses and boundary walls interaction between residents is voluntary. People belong to service, business and different occupations and varying caste groups.

JAWAHAR NAGAR: This housing board colony is at the other extreme, on Agra Road and extends in a big land area divided into seven sectors. The colony has different types and sizes of quarters for low, middle and high income groups. The study covered the low income group quarters situated in a row in a narrow lane. Each house has one room, a small kitchen and a small open area in front. Each house is separated by a common wall and has an identical structure and area, and is occupied by people belonging to the low economic status.

CHANDPOLE BAZAR: This area is situated in the heart of Jaipur city and is surrounded by the city walls. It has a population of 31,049 persons. As a business centre it is highly crowded during the day. After every ten shops is a street, shops are adjacent but partitioned by a common wall. The shops are located on both sides of the entrance to the residential houses whose plinth is a little higher than the shops.

All the houses have common walls with small rooms and low roofs. On the ground floor, every house has some open space which is called a 'Chouck'. Houses are two or three storied. There are no windows in the rooms, or if there are any, they are usually very small and narrow. The terrace is common for all the residents of a house. Three boundary walls are also common for all the households. In almost every house two or more families reside belonging to high, middle and low economic status. Because of the construction of the houses interaction between people is very high.

Sample (Inside Density)

The sample was drawn from the low income group of residents of Jawahar Nagar Housing Board Colony in Jaipur city (see description of area). In terms of space and type of building these houses were identical. The original plan was to select high and low density groups from this colony but sufficient number of houses of low density were not available here. Therefore, subjects for the low density condition were selected from a private colony of similar low income group families where each family occupied space larger than that available in the Housing Board Colony. Thirty male adults from each colony participated in the study. Each family consisted of five to seven members.

Measures and Procedure

SOCIAL BEHAVIOUR AND THE FEELING OF CROWDING: Before the final study thirty adult male residents of a high dense locality were interviewed in an informal setting to assess their feelings and difficulties relating to living in high dense surroundings. On the basis of the information collected through these interviews items were framed in Hindi pertaining to the following areas: feeling towards neighbour, social interaction, physical conditions, encroachment on privacy, feeling of security-insecurity, feeling of crowding, withdrawal from the highly dense conditions and illness.

The questionnaire measure was then given to five experts in psychology and sociology to judge each item for its relevance to day-to-day living in dense environments. The items yielding 100 per cent agreement among the judges were retained. The final form of the questionnaire included 29 items. This questionnaire was administered to an unselected sample of sixty adults from high and low dense areas. The participants were asked to respond on a 4-point rating scale given along with each item ranging from very much (1) to not at all (4). The higher score represented greater negative feeling and vice versa. In case of negative items the scoring was reversed. The total score could range between 29—116. The final version of the questionnaire included items yielding validity indices greater than .20 (for details see Jain, 1983). The questionnaire was individually administered to each participant in one sitting at his residence.

Results

Table 9 shows significant difference in the overall feeling of crowding and social behaviour under low and high inside density conditions. The mean scores were greater for the high inside density group than for the low inside density group. The outside density groups did not differ significantly.

Table 9. Mean Scores on the Feeling of Crowding and Social Behaviour for Outside-Inside Density Groups

Groups		Mean	df	t
OUTSIDE	High density	61.00	98	.49
	Low density	60.00		
INSIDE	High density	89.00	48	7.49**
	Low density	46.70		

** $p < .01$

Table 10 depicts the differences in the feeling of crowding and social behaviours between the two groups. It was observed that high density groups had negative feelings as compared to low density groups on all aspects.

Table 10. Social Behaviours and the Feeling of Crowding Experienced by the
Residents of High and Low Inside Density Conditions

Behaviour/Feeling	Density	Mean	t(48)
Crowding	High	3.55	3.33*
	Low	1.82	
Privacy	High	3.07	3.07*
	Low	1.38	
Physical condition	High	3.22	4.45*
	Low	1.44	
Interaction	High	3.24	3.20*
	Low	1.38	
Neighbours	High	2.65	3.92*
	Low	1.69	
Insecurity	High	2.67	6.5*
	Low	1.24	
Illness	High	3.44	3.39*
	Low	1.71	
Withdrawal	High	3.88	2.43*
	Low	2.46	

*$p < .01$

The results showed that high outside density was not associated
with overall feelings of crowding and negative social behaviour,
whereas the high inside density group showed greater overall feeling
of crowding and negative social behaviour (Table 9). To determine
the specific effects of high inside density further analysis was done
(Table 10). The results consistently showed the negative effects of
high inside density on the feeling of crowding, privacy, perception of
physical conditions, social interaction, liking for neighbour, feeling
of security, health and desire to stay/leave the locality.

The lack of difference in outside density groups may be due to lack
of control over other variables in the field study. Although the two
groups were different in terms of high-low dense localities and similar in SES, number of family members, and accommodation in terms
of number of rooms, the size of the rooms could not be matched. It
is quite possible that the density inside the house may have remained
similar for the two levels of outside density. This possible explanation
is supported by data obtained from inside high-low density groups,
where the high density group showed greater negative effects than the
low density group.

The results are in agreement with the findings of a laboratory study (Griffitt and Veitch, 1971) where high density inside the room was found to be associated with feelings of crowding, negative moods, and affiliative behaviour. Thus inside crowding seems to be more harmful than outside crowding.

Affective Consequences of Population Density

Several studies on the affective state experienced under conditions of high density have been conducted in laboratories and contradictory results have been obtained (Jain, 1987 ;Pandey, 1978). For example, in some studies (Dooley, 1974; Griffitt and Veitch, 1971) intra and interpersonal negative feeling was observed, whereas a strong relationship was not found between density and social interaction by Booth (1976). Why should interpersonal attraction be influenced by high population density? The answer to this question requires some consideration of the bases of interpersonal attraction. Homans (1950) states that the frequency of interaction between two or more persons increases the degree of their liking for one another. In support of this theory Whyte (1956) reported that the overwhelming percentage of co-participants consisted of neighbours, particularly, those who lived next door or across the street. Thus propinquity has been accepted as a necessary condition for interpersonal attraction. High population density provides a condition of propinquity and greater interaction than low population density. Thus, if this theory carries any weight then under the high population density condition the degree of interpersonal attraction should be greater as compared to the low population density condition. Some empirical evidence to this effect comes from an earlier study (Jain, 1976) where greater competition tolerance was observed among the residents of a high dense area compared to their counterparts from a low density area.

In addition to the issue of theory based prediction about interpersonal attraction under high density it is also important to note that different methods are adopted in various cultures to deal with high density living. For instance, the Chinese are reserved and careful in regulating their family life and hence they are not disturbed about living in high density conditions (Mitchel, 1971). The Japanese because of their cultural values adapt to very high densities by 'turning inwards and miniaturising some aspects of their environment (Canter and Canter, 1971). Similarly social withdrawal has been found to be a widespread response to density (Altman and Chemers, 1980).

The present study is aimed at finding out the differences in interpersonal attraction, expected helping, and the feeling of crowding in people under high-low density conditions. In the Indian situation, people from high and low economic status may differ in their responses to high density situations. Therefore, this variable was also taken into account. It was hypothesised that residents of a high density area would show lesser interpersonal attraction and would expect lesser help from neighbours than those from a low density area. Furthermore, the feeling of crowding would be greater in high density and low economic groups than among their counterparts.

Method

Participants

On the basis of census data two localities, *Chandpole* area, and *Shastri Nagar* of Jaipur city were selected as high and low density areas, respectively (descriptions of these areas have already been discussed earlier in this chapter). From each area a group of fifty adult males were drawn and half of them were from the low SES with an annual income up to Rs. 10,000, and the other half belonged to the high SES with an annual income of more than Rs. 30,000. Thus four groups — high density-high income, high density-low income, low density-high income and low density-low income — were formed with twenty-five participants in each group.

Measures

THE INTERPERSONAL JUDGEMENT SCALE: A modified form of the Interpersonal Judgement Scale (IJS) by Byrne (1971), which measures attraction towards a hypothetical stranger, was used. For the present purpose the Hindi version of the 6 items with 7-point scales was prepared and attraction towards neighbours in general was measured.

THE EXPECTED HELPING BEHAVIOUR QUESTIONNAIRE: A 26-item questionnaire was developed by the author. Items included in this questionnaire described situations like accident, financial and social emergency. Along with each described situation were five alternative courses of action. The participants were asked to select any of the alternatives which they expected most of the time.

THE FEELING OF CROWDING RATING SCALE: To assess the degree of the feeling of crowding six bipolar dimensions were used in a semantic differential type rating scale. The dimensions included were : comfortable-uncomfortable, feel bad-feel good, high conges-tion-low congestion, happy-sad, pleasant-unpleasant and negative-positive.

Procedure

The three measures were completed by each participant indi-vidually at his convenience. The order in which the measures were administered remained constant. First the IJS was presented, fol-lowed by the Expected Helping Questionnaire and the Feeling of Crowding Scale.

Results

Table 11 shows that the main effects of density and SES could not reach the significance level on measures of interpersonal attraction as well as on expected helping. However, the trend suggest that the low SES group expressed greater interpersonal attraction than the other groups in the high density condition. The same trend was seen in the case of expected helping. The main effect of density and economic status was significant for the overall feeling of crowding.

It is clear from Table 12 that the high SES participants felt lesser crowding than the low SES participants on all the dimensions except

Table 11. Summary of Main Effects of Density and Economic Status
for Interpersonal Attraction, Expected Helping and the Feeling of Crowding

Dependant Measures	Density			Economic Status		
	Low	High	$F_{(1,96)}$	Low	High	$F_{(1,96)}$
Interpersonal attraction	29.58	28.24	< 1	31.42	26.4	< 1
Expected helping	75.82	72.18	< 1	77.88	70.12	1.10
Feeling of crowding	2.07	2.28	4.84*	2.36	1.99	8.24**

* $p < .05$
** $p < .01$

the feeling of congestion. The overall value of means of high SES
(M = 1.96) and low SES (M = 3.93) were significant. On the other
hand, the high density group differed from the low density group on
three of the six dimensions of the feeling of crowding (Table 13).

Table 12. The Feeling of Crowding in High and Low Economic Status Groups

Dimensions of the Feeling of Crowding	Economic Status	Mean	t (48)
Comfortable-uncomfortable	High	1.97	2.64*
	Low	2.34	
Good-bad	High	1.98	3.57**
	Low	2.48	
High congestion-low congestion	High	2.02	0.32
	Low	2.14	
Happy-sad	High	2.08	2.85**
	Low	2.48	
Pleasant-unpleasant	High	1.86	4.00**
	Low	2.40	
Positive-negative	High	1.86	3.57**
	Low	2.36	

* $p < .05$
** $p < .01$

Table 13. The Feeling of Crowding in High and Low Density Groups

Dimensions of the Feeling of Crowding	Density	Mean	t (48)
Comfortable-uncomfortable	High	2.32	2.28*
	Low	2.00	
Good-bad	High	2.40	2.57**
	Low	2.04	
High congestion-low congestion	High	2.00	0.81
	Low	2.14	
Happy-sad	High	2.38	1.42
	Low	2.18	
Pleasant-unpleasant	High	2.28	2.14*
	Low	1.98	
Positive-negative	High	2.25	1.07
	Low	2.10	

* $p < .05$
** $p < .02$

Discussion

The present findings are not entirely congruent with the findings of Western studies (e.g., Brickman et al, 1973) showing negative effects of high population density on interpersonal attraction and helping behaviour. In view of the present findings related to the economic status it seems that high density in itself is not associated with low degree of attraction towards neighbours. It also depends on the economic status of the individual. Only in the case of low economic status the negative behaviour and feelings in high density situations are aggravated.

The trend which is observed in this study supports proximity as one of the factors necessary for increasing attraction for the residents of a high density area. This is particularly applicable to persons from the low economic status who live in houses which are close to each other and share common spaces. These results are congruent with Festinger, Schachter, and Back's (1950) classic study of friendship and proximity, which also found architectural features to have an important bearing on the social life of residents.

Space is a very important determining factor in interpersonal attraction. However, in high density conditions it is not only the space which increases the interaction but also the insufficiency of resources which compels people to accept help from others. Thus interaction seems to increase interpersonal attraction, and expected help from others seems to maintain it. However, the present study does not provide convincing evidence to this effect.

Greater overall feeling of crowding in a high density area in case of the low economic status group, however, in accordance with Western studies, should have lowered interpersonal attraction and helping behaviour. But the present study does not show unambiguous results. A reasonable speculation in terms of the Indian social set-up does not seem to be out of place. By and large, Indian society emphasises the emotional bonds with relatives, neighbours and with the community. Every one has a social role and responsibility towards others and this concern is reflected in religious preachings and folk wisdom.

The differences between high and low economic groups in terms of the feeling of crowding, interpersonal attraction and expected help are consonant with this kind of reasoning. Persons from the high economic status are perhaps more modernised (in the Western mode of life) than persons from the low economic status.

While discussing the findings in relation to competition tolerance and high density it was suggested (in Chapter 2) that some people develop higher competition tolerance to cope with high density situations characterised by high competition for limited resources. The present findings further lend support to this contention: in the sense that high competition within the high economic group lowers interpersonal attraction and expected help in comparison to the low economic group. In conclusion, it can be stated that economic factors do moderate the effects of high density on social behaviour.

Effects of Crowding on Mental Health

The studies investigating the relationship between population density and mental health have often yielded contradictory results. Evidence in favour of a positive relationship between these variables has been reported in some studies (Bain, 1974; Cox, Paulus, McCain and Karlovac, 1982; Levy and Harzog, 1974; Paulus, McCain and

Cox, 1978; Sengal, 1977) while many studies do not indicate any relationship between population density and mental health (Factor and Waldron, 1973; Golson, 1976; Mitchel, 1971).

It seems that the relationship between population density and its effects on mental health is not straightforward. The reason is that along with population density a host of other factors are necessarily involved which moderate the relationship between population density and human behaviour. Thus population density (physical crowding), although a necessary condition, is in itself not sufficient to create the feeling of crowding. However, if it is perceived as disturbing then the feeling of crowding is more likely to be evoked. Since the feeling of crowding has been perceived as a negative consequence of high population density characterised by stress, discomfort, arousal of control, it is reasonable to postulate that the feeling of crowding leads to negative consequences such as mental health problems. The present study aimed at examining the hypothesis that high population density, if it creates the feeling of crowding, leads to disturbances in mental health. Thus, the feeling of crowding is viewed as an intervening variable between population density and mental health.

Method

Sample

The present study was conducted in a field setting. Two groups of a hundred adult males drawn from high-low density areas in Bikaner, Rajasthan participated in the study. These groups were more or less matched in terms of socio-economic status, size of family, duration of residence, material facilities and cultural artifacts (e.g., refrigerator, fans and radios) available in the house.

Measures

MEASURE OF DAY-TO-DAY FEELINGS: This measure was developed by the author (Jain, 1983) to assess the feeling of crowding characterised by the perception of crowding, feelings of insecurity,

anxiety, withdrawal, negative attitudes towards neighbours, distur-
bance of noise, uncleanliness and lack of space. Items pertaining to
these areas were rated on a 4-point scale (for details see Jain, 1983).

KEY INFORMANT SCHEDULE: This schedule developed by
Gahlot, Gautam and Gupta (1983), deals with the measure of mental
illness in various diagnostic categories. It contains details of
background information and items related to the symptoms of various diagnostic categories of mental illness.

Procedure

Each participant was individually contacted at his residence and
the feeling of crowding questionnaire was administered. On the basis
of the median scores on the measure of the feeling of crowding, the
participants were divided into two groups: high feeling of crowding
and low feeling of crowding. The Key Informant Schedule was
administered individually to the participants in both the groups.

Results

Table 14 shows the difference between the high-low crowding
groups on various aspects of day-to-day feelings. The two groups

Table 14. Feelings Expressed by High Crowding and Low Crowding Groups

Feeling	High Crowding	Low Crowding	t (198)
Security-insecurity	8.28	4.14	16.65
Towards neighbours	11.29	65.87	18.17
Withdrawal	6.82	4.31	9.46
Loud noise	8.30	3.43	18.27
Illness	5.82	4.01	9.10
Anxiety	8.57	4.23	16.32
Dirty surroundings	6.25	2.38	19.24
Congestion	13.4	5.73	22.75

Note: All t values are significant, $p < .01$. Lower scores mean more
positive feeling.

differed significantly on all the aspects of day-to-day feelings. The high crowding group expressed greater feeling of crowding than the low crowding group.

Table 15 depicts the number of persons in each group showing various types of mental health problems. The two groups showed differences on all the problems.

Table 15. Types of Mental Illness in High and Low Crowding Groups

Types of Mental Illness	High Crowding Group	Low Crowding Group
General mental health	66	37
Schizophrenia	18	5
Depression	43	10
Anxiety	20	11
Organic Brain Syndrome	16	3
Paranoid	7	–
Obsessive Compulsive Neuroses	11	–
Alcoholism	10	5
Hysteria/epilepsy	5	1
Mania	10	7
Phobia	9	3
Mental retardation	8	1

Discussion

The hypothesis proposed at the beginning of this study was supported by the results which clearly showed a significantly greater feeling of crowding and incidence of mental health problems in the high dense group than in the low dense group.

This difference could be accounted for. by the fact that as the number of persons in a given space increases, so do social obligations and the need to inhibit individual desires. This escalation of both social demands and the need to inhibit desires results in the feeling of being cramped and of not having enough space. This gives rise to the feeling of crowding resulting in mental illness. It appears that when the amount of space available per person is less, there arises a psychological state of discomfort associated with wanting more space than is available. Thus, it seems reasonable to expect that people react to incessant demands. stimulations, and lack of privacy, etc., resulting from overcrowding with irritability, withdrawal, weariness, etc. Moreover, high crowding tends to intensify the usual reactions to a social situation and leads to mental illness.

This study shows the importance of psychological evaluation of high density situations in producing negative consequences. The earlier studies have not taken into account the mediating factor, viz., the feeling of crowding while assessing the relationship between density and mental health. The importance of cognitive factors in stress is evident in this study as it is the feeling of crowding which is found to be associated with mental illness and not population density *per se*. The results, however, do not warrant any causal relationship between the feeling of crowding and mental health, but support the studies where health problems were found to be associated with crowding (e.g., Cox, Paulus and McCain, 1984).

— 4 —

Experimental Verification of Crowding

The studies reported in the preceding chapters are by and large of a correlational nature which have inherent limitations in uncovering the causal links between the antecedents and consequences of crowding. Also, they tell very little about the processes through which population density affects the feeling of crowding as well as other aspects of behaviour. We will discuss some studies where efforts have been made to identify the salient variables responsible for the affective and behavioural consequences of crowding in experimental situations.

The results presented earlier suggest that scarcity of resources, a characteristic of an individual of low economic status, and competition for goal attainment contribute relatively more to the negative effects of high population density. In order to test this assumption a series of experiments were designed with a focus on the issue of resources and the feeling of crowding. In addition, the problem of personal space and attribution of discomfort, arising out of congestion in high density, were also examined. The three studies presented in this chapter share one basic premise that high density creates a situation of congestion where the likelihood of invasion of personal space is greater and that the presence of a large number of persons is associated with scarcity of resources.

Personal Space: An Attributional Analysis of Crowding

The concept of personal space was first introduced by Hall (1966), which stimulated a lot of research on the determinants of interpersonal distance one likes to maintain in different situations. Altman and Vinsel (1977) reviewed studies on personal space and indicated a need for studying intercultural differences regarding personal space. At present, the concept of personal space has been criticised by many researchers (e.g., Lecuyer, 1976 cited in Claude Levy-Leboyer; Canter and Griffiths, 1982) on the ground that nothing can be predicted about the reactions to intrusion without considering the situation. It is, therefore, suggested that researchers should concentrate on interpersonal distance as a measure of personal space. Interpersonal distance (or personal space) can also be dictated by the situational constraints. For example, in high density interpersonal distance is bound to decrease.

It is intuitively clear that high population density increases the likelihood of intrusion into one's personal space. Worchel and Teddlie (1976) have argued that intrusion of personal space can be stressful under high density only when the cause of intrusion is attributed to intruders. It seems that the effects of violation of personal space are similar to the effects of crowding on social interaction and task performance. It can be suggested that high population density and the feeling of crowding emerge because of violation of personal space. However, Worchel (1978) has shown that attributional processes are much more important for the feeling of crowding than for the invasion on personal space. Increasing concern with cognitive factors underlying environmental stress has led investigators to examine the role of attributions in arousal in high density situations (Patterson, 1973; Worchel and Yohai, 1979) in determining the experience of crowding. Worchel, Brown and Webb (1983) investigated the effects of manipulation of the subjects' perception of control on stress during crowding. They found that maximum stress occurred in the condition of control over one of the variables. It was also observed that in this situation subjects perceived their arousal as being caused by a controllable stimulus.

According to the theory of personal space and attribution (Worchel, 1978), the feeling of crowding is conceived as a two-stage phenomenon. The individual is first aroused by violations of his personal space; he then seeks to explain why he is aroused. Thus arousal due to violation of personal space and attribution of the cause of arousal are important determinants of the feeling of crowding. Extending Worchel's (1978) model the present study explored the role of attribution in creating the feeling of crowding. More specifically, this study examined the feeling of crowding, task performance, and decision-making, under varying levels of density in distracted and non-distracted conditions. It was expected that greater feeling of crowding would be seen under the high dense low distracted condition than under the non-distracted condition.

Method

Design

The experiment employed a 2 x 2 factorial design with two levels of density (high/low) and two levels of distraction (non-distraction/distraction).

Sample

The study was conducted on a hundred female tenth grade students randomly drawn from several schools. Their age ranged from 14.6 to 19 years. The subjects were equally and randomly assigned to the four treatment conditions.

Measures

ANAGRAM TASK: Anagrams involve transposition of alphabets of a word to form a new word. A set of twelve Hindi anagrams were used to assess task performance. These anagrams were selected according to the knowledge of participants and were pre-tested on a small sample. For example, alphabets like 'M A R S H C R A T P' had to be rearranged to form a meaningful word, 'SAMACHAR PATR' in *Hindi*.

PUNITIVE JUDGEMENT: A hypothetical story highlighting the undesirable behaviour of the hero (a boy) was prepared. The partici-pants were asked to read the story and decide on the degree of punish-ment, which they thought, should be given to the hero. The decision regarding the punishment was made on a 7-point scale ranging from highest punishment (7) through no punishment (4) to reward (1).

THE FEELING OF CROWDING: The feeling of crowding was measured using the items related to feelings towards the experiment, the experimenter, the room, colleagues and self mood. Such measures have been frequently used in crowding research (e.g., Griffitt and Veitch, 1971). Each item depicted a question about how the subject felt about the behaviour of the experimenter during the experiment (questions were related to each of the feeling objects). These feelings were rated on two 5-point scales anchored with a positive and nega-tive adjective (e.g., very good-very bad, very interesting-very un-interesting). The scores on all the scales were summed up to get a single score for the feeling of crowding. The minimum and maximum score ranges from 10 to 50. The higher scores represent greater feeling of crowding.

Procedure

The experiment was conducted on a group of twenty-five par-ticipants at a time. One of the rooms in which the experiment was conducted was 12′ × 30′ in size and represented the low density condition. The other room was 18' × 10' in size and represented the high density condition. The seating arrangement was oval shaped. For creating a distraction condition a tape recorder with a dummy mike was placed in the room and subjects were informed that the tape recorder and mike would record the deliberations of the session. Apart from the size of the room and the presence or absence of the distractor, the procedural aspects were identical across all the four conditions. After the participants had occupied their seats in the room a booklet containing the anagram task was distributed to them. The instructions were read out and a demonstration was given to solve anagrams. Then the participants were asked to complete all the twelve anagrams as quickly as possible. It took them about half an hour to complete the task, following which they were asked to turn the page of the booklet which contained a short story. They were asked to read the story carefully and then give their suggestions regarding the treatment that the hero of the story should be given. They were asked to tick off any one of the seven treatments listed on the response sheet. When the subjects had completed this task they were asked to turn to the third page of the booklet and read the instructions carefully. The subjects were requested to express their feelings towards the experiment, the experimenter, the room, colleagues and self mood. After completion of this task the booklets were collected and participants were thanked for their cooperation and the experiment was terminated. This procedure was followed in all the four conditions of the experiment.

Results

The scores on the dependent measures, i.e., anagram task, punitive judgement, and the feeling of crowding were separately subjected to 2 × 2 factorial analysis of variance. Significant main effect of density was obtained on the measure of task performance $F(1,21) = 11.55$, $p < .01$. The high density condition yielded a lower level of performance (M = 4) than the low density condition (M = 6.6). Similarly the main effect of distraction on task performance was also significant $F(1,21) = 4.99$, $p < .05$. The distracting situation led to a lower level of performance (M = 4.09) than the non-distraction condition

(M = 5.8). The interaction of the two variables did not reach the significance level $F(1,21) = 1, p > .05$.

The ANOVA for the measures of punitiveness yielded significant main effect of density and distraction variables. For density, $F(1,21) = 4.33, p < .05$ and distraction, $F(1,21) = 6.23, p < .05$.

The participants in the high density situation suggested greater punishment (M = 3.32) than those in the low density condition (M=2.08). The interaction effects of the two variables were not significant, $F(1,21) = 1, p > .05$. In the distraction condition subjects suggested more punitive action (M = 3.60) than in the non-distraction situation (M=3.13).

The results pertaining to the feeling of crowding showed significant main effect of distraction $F(1,21)=6.88, p < .01$ and density $F(1,21) = 5.88, p < .05$. The high density condition led to a greater feeling of crowding (M=21.18) than the low density condition (M=19.72). Similarly the feeling of crowding was more in non-distracted (M=19.66) than in distracted condition (M=18.20). The interaction effect was also significant $F(1,21)=4.38, p < .05$, suggesting greater difference between the distraction and non-distraction groups in the high density condition on the feeling of crowding as compared to that between the two groups in the low density condition.

Discussion

As expected the findings of this study demohstı ated that distraction from the source of crowding stress would ameliorate the feeling of crowding. However, the present findings are not unequivocal since punitiveness was observed more in the distraction rather than in the non-distraction condition (Worchel, 1978). Thus, the feeling of crowding can be considered as due to violation of personal space and attribution of violation to the presence of a large number of individuals in the same space.

The decrement of performance under distraction further supports the significance of attribution in creating the feeling of crowding stress. To this extent Worchel's (1978) findings are in consonance with the present observations.

Reduced punitive actions in the non-distraction condition is not in line with the aforesaid model. It seems as though along with distraction the participants became more cautious in suggesting punishment for the guilty. However, no specific explanation can be given for this inconsistency. One source may be the female subjects studied in this investigation. The theory, however, does not predict any sex differences. Some findings have been reported about consistent sex differences in the responses to higher density. Females are generally found to express lesser degree of the feeling of crowding than males. The overall findings support the process of attribution leading to the feeling of crowding. Another important question remains to be answered and that is the role of personal space in the feeling of crowding. The subsequent study is related to this issue.

Effects of Population Density on Personal Space

For the analysis of environment-behaviour relationship Altman and Chemers (1980) proposed a social systems orientation where privacy was viewed as the central organising factor. Within this framework a series of behavioural mechanisms have been suggested to attain the momentary desired level of privacy. One of these mechanisms is maintaining personal space, or the 'invisible boundary' surrounding a person (Sommer, 1969). Studies on personal space have shown that violations of personal space produce discomfort and arousal (Hall, 1966; Sommer, 1969). Personal space has been found to be associated with arousal and crowding (Epstein and Karlin, 1975). Earlier research on population density, however, has been inconclusive since social density leads to certain forms of behaviour and spatial density leads to other forms of behaviour (Worchel, 1978). Stokols (1972) has suggested that density and crowding are two distinct concepts and that they are not always related to each other. Recently, Worchel (1978) has presented evidence that it is personal space and not density which leads to the feeling of crowding. Thus, personal space and density are treated differently to influence behaviour under some conditions and not under others.

Hayduck (1983) has cited a variety of data to the effect that spatial preferences are sensitive to physical settings. Aiello, DeRist, Epstein and Karlin (1977) have examined the role of personal space as a mediator of short-term crowding involving close interpersonal proximity. They found that subjects who preferred greater interpersonal distance were more stressed.

Studies on crowding have reported different mediators between density and the feeling of crowding; e.g., competition for space (Epstein and Karlin, 1975); competition tolerance (Jain, 1978); loss of control over interactions (Ruback and Carr, 1984); scarcity of resources (Jain, 1983; McCallum, Rusbult, Hong, Walden and Schopler, 1979), stimulus overload (Milgram, 1970); and invasion of privacy (Altman and Chemers, 1980). Interpersonal distance has also been considered as one of the antecedents of the feeling of crowding in high density conditions (Sundstrom, 1978).

By and large, earlier research on personal space has been concerned with examining the effects of factors such as age, sex (Tennis and Dabbas, 1975), social-emotional disorders (Horowitz, Dutt and Stratlon, 1964) and situational variables (Bass and Weinstein, 1971). Attempts have also been made to manipulate personal space to see its effect on an individual's perceptions of others (e.g., Konecni, Libuser, Mortan and Ebbesen, 1975).

Findings on personal space and interaction distance may eventually be linked with the effects of crowding as it is under high density conditions that the probability of violation of personal space increases. But the differential effects of crowding and personal space have been relatively ignored by the researchers. Some of the researchers have gone to the extent of accepting crowding as an invasion of personal space (e.g., Evans, 1978). The effects of individual differences in personal space on social behaviour are not fully understood. Dooley (1974) found that in high density conditions *far personal space men* (subjects who desired greater distance with others) felt more unfriendly toward others and more negative and irritable than *close personal space men* (subjects who desired lesser distance with others). On the other hand, Loo (1972) did not observe these effects in children.

It appears from these studies that when personal space is used as an independent variable the effects on behaviour are similar to the effects of crowding. For example, encroachment of personal space (or the feeling of crowding) may create differential effects on behaviour such as eye contact (Sommer, 1969), task performance (Rawls, Trego,

McGaffery and Rawls, 1972), and arousal (Evans, 1978). Worchel and Teddlie (1976) have perceived encroachment of personal space as the first stage of the feeling of crowding and some support for this has been obtained in the preceding study. However, when personal space is regarded as a dependent variable its antecedents may be quite different from those of the feeling of crowding. Thus, the concept of personal space poses complexity in understanding its specific consequences as well as its relationship with the feeling of crowding.

Against this background, the present study experimentally examined the proposition that encroachment of personal space is associated with social interaction. If an individual's interaction in a density situation is controlled then high density should not lead to the feeling of invasion of personal space. In his previous work the author (Jain, 1984) found that non-interaction in a high density situation produces the feeling of crowding. Considering the interrelationship between personal space and crowding it was hypothesised that non-interaction in a high density condition would create a desire for greater personal space than under a low density condition. In addition, it was also expected that interpersonal distance would be greater for an unfamiliar than for a familiar stimulus person.

Method

Design

The experiment involved a 2 × 2 factorial design with two levels of spatial density (low/high) and two types of stimulus person (familiar/unfamiliar). The second factor was replicated for the subjects. The rooms of high and low density were 5.85 m^2 and 16.72 m^2 with density .77 m^2 and 1.76 m^2 per person, respectively.

Participants

Forty female post-graduate students of Rajasthan University, Jaipur participated in the study. Their ages ranged from 22 to 24 years

(M=22.60). They were randomly assigned to the two treatment conditions, in each condition there were twenty subjects. Both the groups were exposed to familiar and unfamiliar stimulus person conditions.

Measures

PERSONAL SPACE: The Inter Personal Comfortable Scale (ICDS) of Veitch, Gestinger and Arkkalin (1976) was used to measure personal space. It consisted of a circle 18 cm in diameter with eight arms drawn from the centre. Each subject was required to mark on each arm the point at which he would like to stop the other person approaching him. The marked distances on all the eight arms were added and averaged to obtain a single score.

EXPERIMENTAL TASK: The geometrical figures were prepared in such a manner that each drawing involved the use of a compass, a scale, a ruler, and an eraser. These figures consisted of circles, triangles, lines, and arcs. The pre-testing phase established that drawing all the figures required about 20 minutes on an average. The task did not involve any interaction among the participants.

Procedure

The experiment involved four conditions. Initially all the participants of a group were invited in to the room and asked to sit on chairs arranged in the room. The participants in all the conditions were told that they would be given a test to assess the ability of space perception and skill of drawing figures. Each subject was given experimental materials which were placed on a small table in front of her chair. They were instructed to complete the task within a period of 20 minutes. Participants were asked to copy all the figures with the help of material on their table. Each drawing was supposed to be an exact replica of the original one. The participants were asked to finish the task accurately and neatly. The drawing sheets were collected after 20 minutes. Thereafter, the subjects received the ICDS with the prescribed instructions. They were asked to imagine a stranger/familiar girl coming towards them, and to mark the distance they would like to stop her so that they felt comfortable.

Results

The main effect of spatial density was significant for personal space $F(1,76) = 11.49, p < .01$. Greater interpersonal distance was desired under high (M = 15.245) than under low spatial density condition (M = 13.375). Similarly the main effect of familiarity with the stimulus person was significant $F(1,76) = 67.96, p < .01$. The desired interpersonal distance was greater for an unfamiliar (M = 16.50) than for a familiar person (M = 12.05). The interaction of familiarity and density was also significant $F(1,76) = 4.45, p < .05$. The difference between unfamiliar and familiar stimulus person conditions for desired distance was greater in high (M = 5.64) than in low density condition (M = 3.35).

Discussion

The results supported the hypothesis that high density is associated with personal space and greater personal space is desired for unfamiliar than for familiar persons. The results are also in agreement with studies considering personal space as a concomitant of high density (Sundstrom, 1978). It seems that high density as a spatial antecedent of the feeling of crowding also works as a stressor for personal space. Both personal space and high density can be considered as spatial factors associated with the feeling of crowding.

The feeling of crowding as an affective component of stress motivates people to reduce or to avoid such conditions which produce these feelings, such as high density and close proximity with others. The anticipated presence of a large number of people have been reported to produce the feeling of crowding (Baum and Koman, 1976). In the present study mere presence of a large number of persons (high density) without involving any interaction produced discomfort. Thus closer distance was not desired by subjects in the high density condition. It seems that high density not only creates the feeling of crowding (Jain, 1983) but also instigates people to reduce stress by desiring greater interpersonal distance. The results suggest that density can be considered as a stressor (Booth, 1976; Galle, Gove and McPherson, 1972; Worchel, 1978). The obtained insignificant interaction between density and familiarity suggests that high density creates stress in terms of personal space.

It seems that violation of personal space can be felt by individuals even in the absence of interaction and, thus, mere close proximity with others acts as a stressor to arouse (Evans, 1978) which, in turn, leads to the feeling of crowding. Feeling of encroachment of personal space, and not objective spatial distance, seems to be the necessary and sufficient condition for the feeling of crowding. Further research, however, is needed to test this hypothesis where non-interaction and interaction situations can be compared for the feeling of invasion.

This study has suggested that under the high density condition both the feeling of crowding and the desire for greater interpersonal distance are reported. High density in the Indian context is associated with low resources as has been shown in the studies reported here. Therefore, it will be interesting to know whether in the experimental condition scarcity of resources along with high density produces the feeling of crowding and the desire for greater interpersonal distance. The subsequent study explores this possibility.

Effects of Density and Resources on Crowding and Personal Space

Research on population density has generally maintained the distinction between physical density and the psychological state of crowding. As Stokols (1972) has suggested perceptions of crowding involve a negative affective state rather than mere report of density. This distinction is useful in handling the contradictory findings in the area of population density (e.g., Aiello, Vautier and Bernstein, 1983; Marshall and Heslin, 1975; Freedman, Klevansky and Ehrlich, 1971). It has been observed that physical density may or may not lead to the feeling of crowding and negative effects on behaviour (Stokols, 1978a) depending upon several variables such as the relationship between members, quality of environment, the nature of the task, and the purpose involved in the interaction. A majority of the studies demonstrate the adverse effects of crowding on behaviour. However, only scant attention has been paid to the specific factors associated with density which determine the feeling of crowding. The theoretical explanations put forward to explain the experience of crowding under high density situations emphasise various factors such as excessive arousal, lack of control and scarcity of resources (Stokols, 1978a). The only common factor seems to be the negative perception of the situation as interfering with the individual's pursuit of his goals. Thus any factor perceived as goal blocking can trigger off the feeling of crowding. Which of the factors would be considered negative, depends on the situational factors, the socio-cultural context, and the frequency of this incidence. The significance of perception in the feeling of crowding has been noted by Worchel (1978) in his two-factor attribution model of crowding.

In India high population density is pervasive and is associated with scarcity of resources. Scarcity of resources includes both spatial restrictions and also other physical amenities of everyday life. A recent study has shown that individuals of low economic status gave greater negative affective responses in a high dense locality than individuals of high economic status (Preet and Jain, 1984). The ecological model of crowding also conceives scarcity of resources as the chief factor underlying the feeling of crowding. In a laboratory study (McCallum, Rusbult, Hong, Walden and Schopler, 1979) scarcity of resources was manipulated by varying the size of the group and hence the effect of group size and resources could not be separated. Both, high density and scarcity of resources constitute conditions of high competition. The former increases competition because of the presence of other individuals and the latter because of the paucity of resources. Therefore, the two variables (density and resources) might yield similar effects on the feeling of crowding.

The present study explored the effects of high density and scarcity of resources, both seen frequently in cosmopolitan Indian towns, on the feeling of crowding and personal space. It was predicted that high density and scarcity of resources result in greater feeling of crowding, than low density and adequate resources. In addition, the effect of both these variables on personal space was determined to see whether the effect of scarcity of resources on the feeling of crowding could also be attributed to the invasion of personal space. It was assumed that under high density and scarce resource conditions individuals would like to maintain greater interpersonal comfortable distance than under low density and adequate resource conditions. Two separate experiments were conducted to study these issues under social and spatial density conditions.

Experiment 1

This experiment examined the effect of social density and resources on the feeling of crowding and personal space. Social density was created by varying the number of persons and keeping the living space constant. This experiment used a 2 × 2 factorial design with two levels of social density (high/low) and two levels of resources (adequate/scarce).

Method

PARTICIPANTS: Forty post-graduate female students participated in the study. Their ages ranged between 22 to 24 years (M = 23.40 years). They were randomly assigned to the four conditions of the experiment. The high and low density conditions had fifteen and five subjects respectively.

PROCEDURE: The experiment involved four conditions, namely, high density-scarce resources, high density-adequate resources, low density-scarce resources, and low density-adequate resources. Initially all the subjects of a group were invited in to the room and asked to sit on the chairs arranged in the room. The experimental room was 8.5′ × 11′ in area. In high and low density conditions population density was 8.23 and 18.70 square feet per person, respectively. The participants in the adequate resources conditions received a compass, a ruler, an eraser, a drawing sheet, a pencil, and a chart showing ten geometrical figures, whereas in the scarce resources conditions they received only a pencil, a drawing sheet, and a figure chart. The participants in all the conditions were informed that they would be given a test to assess their ability concerning space perception and their skill in drawing figures. The experimental materials were placed on a small table just in front of each participant's chair. She was instructed to complete the task within 20 minutes. She was asked to copy all the drawings using the material given to her. Each drawing was supposed to be the replica of the figure on the chart. The subjects were asked to finish the task with complete accuracy and neatness and not to talk to any one while working.

The drawing sheets were collected after 20 minutes. Thereafter, the participants received the ICDS with the required instructions. They were asked to imagine a strange girl coming towards them. Having completed the scale, the participants completed the feeling of crowding measure. When they finished their task they were thanked and asked to disperse.

Results

The ANOVA performed on the scores on the measures of the feeling of crowding yielded a significant main effect of social density $F(1,36) = 33.38$, $p < .01$. The participants reported less amount of crowding under low (M = 141.10) than high (M = 115.3) density conditions. The main effect of resources also reached the significance level $F(1,36) = 7.96$, $p < .01$, with lesser feeling of crowding under adequate (M = 134.50) than scarce (M = 121.90) resource conditions. The measure of personal space did not yield any significant effect of density but the main effect of resources was significant $F(1,36) = 18.25$, $p < .01$. The adequate resources condition led to lesser amount of desired comfortable distance (M = 2.27) than scarce resources condition (M = 2.71). The interaction of social density and resources was not significant for both the measures, for the feeling of crowding $F(1,36) = 3.73$ and for personal space $F(1,36) = .28$, $p < .05$.

Discussion

The results support the predictions that high social density leads to a greater feeling of crowding as compared to low density. This finding is consonant with the findings reported in other studies (e.g., Baron, Mendel, Adams and Griffen 1976, Saegert, 1974). However, the effect of social density on personal space was not significant, hence no support was obtained for the assumption made by Stokols (1978a). The feeling of crowding in high density may be due to the physical condition of high density itself as the situation of the present experiment required each participant to do her task on her table; hence, other verbal or behavioural interactions were absent. The second prediction that the scarce resources condition would also lead to a greater feeling of crowding and desire for greater interpersonal distance compared to the adequate resources condition was confirmed. Thus, the feeling of crowding seems to be the independent product of density and resources. But, why do scarce resources result in the increment of personal space? This question may be answered in terms of attribution of the stress created by scarce resources to the presence of so many others (Worchel, Brown and Webb, 1983). It was also expected that density and resources would show an interactive effect on both the variables, but the prediction was not confirmed. It seems that the negative feeling of crowding can be felt because of independent stressors such as high density and scarce resources, probably due to increased competition in both the situations.

Experiment 2

This experiment was designed to test a hypothesis similar to the one in Experiment 1 with a difference—instead of social density, spatial density was manipulated by varying the space and keeping the number of persons constant. The purpose was to determine whether the type of density makes any difference in the effects of these variables on the feeling of crowding. The two conditions were different in terms of group size and similar in terms of density per square feet.

Method

PARTICIPANTS: Forty post-graduate female students enrolled at Rajasthan University, Jaipur, participated in this experiment. Their ages ranged between 22 to 24 years (M = 22.6 years). They were randomly assigned to the four experimental conditions with ten participants in each cell of the design. In the high density condition the size of the experimental room was 7' × 9' with a density of 8.3 square feet per person and for low density 15' × 12' with density of 18.9 square feet per person.

MEASURES: The measures of the feeling of crowding and interpersonal comfortable distance used in Experiment 1 were also used in this experiment.

PROCEDURE: The procedure and the measures were the same as those used in Experiment 1.

Results

ANOVA revealed that the main effect of spatial density was significant for the feeling of crowding $F(1,36)=16.29$, $p<.01$. Greater feeling of crowding was observed under high (M=141.5) than low (M=153.30) spatial density. Similarly the main effect of resources on the feeling of crowding was significant $F(1,36) = 11.92, p < .01$. The feeling of crowding was greater under the scarce resources condition (M=140.80) than under the adequate resources condition (M=151.55). The main effect of density was significant for personal space $F(1,36)=100.63$, $p<.01$. The desire for greater interpersonal comfortable distance was found under high spatial density (M=1.85) than low density condition (M=1.55). Similarly greater distance was recorded in scarce (M=1.825) than adequate (M=1.53) resources condition $F(1,36) = 87.12, p < .01$. The interaction was non-significant for both the measures; for the feeling of crowding, $F(1,36)=.84$ and for personal space, $F(1,36) = .62, p>.05$.

Discussion

The results supported the hypothesis that high spatial density as well as scarce resources lead to the feeling of crowding, and create a desire to maintain greater distance between oneself and strangers (Epstein and Karlin, 1975; Sundstrom, 1975). Since both the variables (spatial density and scarce resources) had similar effects on the feeling of crowding and personal space, it can be argued that the feeling of crowding was not generated by density alone but also by scarcity of resources. Scarcity of resources seems to be an important non-spatial variable responsible for the feeling of crowding. These two variables did not interact with each other to influence the affective response.

General Discussion

The findings of the two experiments suggest that population density in its social or spatial form is associated with the feeling of crowding. The presence of other persons in a smaller space while performing a task, even in the absence of verbal and behavioural interactions, created the feeling of crowding. Perhaps the absence of interaction between density and resources is due to the individual's belief that scarcity of resources is because of a larger number of people who compete for the available resources. This belief may lead attribution of stress of scarcity or high density to a common factor, i.e., larger number of individuals. The presence of any one of the factors, therefore, seems to be sufficient to produce the feeling of crowding and desire for greater personal space. Whether the present findings can be generalised to other societies where people do not have frequent experiences of high density along with scarce resources as observed in India is yet to be explored.

In general, the present results are in line with the ecological model of crowding in the sense that scarcity of resources is associated with the feeling of crowding. However, scarcity of resources does not seem to mediate between high population density and the feeling of crowding, rather it influences the affective feeling independently but in a way similar to density. Theoretically, high population density can be characterised as a state of scarce resources. According to this viewpoint, high population density seems to provide stress on competition for the utilisation of resources. Perhaps this is the reason that high population density is conducive to produce competition tolerance as a coping strategy to live in such a situation (Jain, 1978). The similarity of the results of the two experiments have indicated the importance of scarce resources in accentuating the feeling of crowding.

—5—

An Overview

The environment provides the experiential base of human life, and, also makes provisions for the enactment of different behaviours and skills. The nature, intensity, and quality of transactions between human beings and the environment largely depend upon the capacities and capabilities of human beings for behavioural functions. While the environment sets the limits for human behaviour, human beings substantially contribute to the quality of the environment. Human curiosity, potential and desire to enhance self-efficacy have been constantly changing the features of the human environment, which is treated as a resource to be consumed and exploited by human beings. It was rarely viewed as a partner of equal status deserving care. The consequence of this attitude has been the destruction of the human environment in different forms.

The dimensions and qualities of the environment in which we now live are largely determined by different types of human interventions. Human beings first make the environment and are then governed by it. Built environment creates various unwanted and unforeseen problems for human beings who shape the environment for their own convenience. How the built environment dictates human behaviour has been shown by Barker (1968) in his famous work on 'behaviour setting'. Recent research has shown that architectural designs of houses or hospitals facilitate certain behaviours and inhibit others. Even the arrangement of the furniture inside the house has been found to be associated with the moods of the residents.

The complexity of man-environment relationship is further increased by social and cultural norms. It has been recognised in the interaction model of personality that a constant interplay between personality make-up and situational demands determines behaviour. The environmental beliefs, attitudes, personal goals, and cognitive ability, on the person side and characteristics of the physical environment, on the other, interactively determine the behavioural outcomes.

The effects of human beings are towards optimisation of the environment so that their needs are fulfilled, their goals are achieved and they are able to pursue their desired activities. To accomplish this goal they exploit the environment and an unending cycle is thus created.

One of the most difficult aspects of this situation is the unprecedented growth in population. Most developing countries are facing the problem of population management. The dynamics of population behaviour are being studied from several perspectives. Since population grows not only in size but also in density, it creates a peculiar problem of adjustment in which human beings have to cope with the stresses created by the presence of other fellow beings. The study of crowding from the psychological perspective tries to answer some of the questions pertaining to the threats emerging from crowding and challenges involved in its moderation, reduction and channelisation.

Conclusions and Implications

The present work has tried to characterise the experiences and consequences of crowding in different spheres of life, in laboratory as well as in field settings. The theoretical framework in which these studies were framed and pursued is one which views crowding as an emotional stress experienced in a specific cultural context having bearings on resource management. The available models have largely confined themselves to variables in an isolated manner and have largely been developed in the West where the magnitude of crowding is lower and societal conditions are different from those faced in developing South Asian countries. This difference needs to be understood because traditional societies enjoy different sets of values and norms governing interpersonal relationships. Indian society, in particular, cherishes dependence and interdependence rather than independence, and relationships are found to be more important than task considerations (J.B.P. Sinha, 1968, 1970, 1985). The linkages with extended families which involve living together of many individuals, often from different generations, makes the situation different from the individualistic lifestyle of the West.

Against this background the present work, in a series of interrelated experiments and field studies, has tried to empirically examine the effects of high density situations on certain aspects of behaviour and to isolate the components of density responsible for the adverse effects. High density was found to be related to greater competition tolerance which reflects a positive motivational capacity to lead life in order to achieve higher material goals. But in a resource limited society how many persons will be able to attain the desired goals and for how long will they be able to sustain high tolerance? These questions become more important in a society which is in a transitional phase of its journey from traditional values to modern values. The intervening junction in this process is quite stressful where the direction of the future path is largely undecided. At the individual level, therefore, perception of high density as a source of stress becomes salient for generating the feeling of crowding. Abject poverty, increasing slums and high density of population in India, have created a situation of helplessness and loss of control over the environment and people have lost the desire to improve the quality of life. This cognitive appraisal of the stressor, in Cohen's (1980) view, is the key to understanding and planning research on crowding. The present study has revealed that competition tolerance motivates an individual to compete with others whether the 'others' are from an in-group (homogeneous) or from an out-group (heterogeneous). This reflects the transitory phase of society in which high density conditions and limited resources have forced individuals to keep away the traditional values of in-group considerations, at least in the fields where competition is inevitable. Higher education has been found to be related with high competition tolerance suggesting that greater awareness of one's environment creates greater arousal, which, after a certain limit of tolerance may produce stresses (Evans, 1978).

The study of social behaviour has revealed the importance of socio-cultural factors in the perception of stress and its consequences at the affective and behavioural levels. The high density environment, particularly inside dwelling units, was found to be associated with the feeling of crowding, lack of privacy, insecurity, and withdrawal. This clearly supports the view that limited resources (in terms of low economic status) and high density are perceived by people from the low economic status as stressful. Withdrawal response in high density situations is noted in many cultures (Altman and Chemers, 1980). However, in the present context withdrawal was reported only as a desire. Since low economic status people do not have resources to change their living standards, this is a state of helplessness and of loss of control over the circumstances. In a way the consequences of high density stress are more evident at the feeling level. The present study does not preclude the behavioural consequences of crowding stress. However, at both the objective and subjective levels, because of the unprecedented growth of population, it is difficult to improve upon the adverse circumstances, particularly in the case of low economic status people. It would, therefore, be interesting to explore the coping strategies adopted by such people.

The present study also investigated crowding stress in relation to different levels of socio-economic status. Interpersonal attraction, and expected helping was almost similar across the residents of high-low density areas as well as across high-low status groups. In contrast, the feeling of crowding varied as a function of density and economic status. Low economic status people felt greater crowding than those from high economic strata. These results suggest the significance of socio-cultural factors in creating the experience of crowding. In spite of the stress, expressed in terms of greater experience of crowding in high density conditions by low economic status people, the consequences remained at the feeling level. Concern with neighbours and others remain intact even under stressful conditions, which is perhaps because of the social mores and obligations which Indian's share and practice in social interactions. These findings are contrary to Western studies, and the differences are likely to be culturally specific. Another important aspect of the findings is that living with stress may lead to adaptation to stress conditions and the apparent negative consequences may not be observed at the level of social interaction.

Does coping with stress or the absence of behavioural manifestation at the social level have no psychological cost? The answer to this question is probably in the negative as has been indicated in the study of crowding and mental health. The higher incidence of mental health problems in high crowding groups suggests that the feeling of crowding, a product of high density condition, is stress producing.

High density as perceived stress leading to adverse consequences on feeling and behaviour has also been reported in the preceding chapter. Scarcity of resources, even in the absence of interactions, has been found to be a source of stress independent of high density. High social as well as spatial density was found more stressful under scarce resource conditions. The feeling of crowding appears to be a perceptual-cognitive one in which scarcity of resources and invasion of personal space are considered as stresses. Since scarcity of resources produces competition, persons, even in the absence of high density, want to maintain relatively greater interpersonal distance with strangers. However, in case of familiar persons the desired personal space is comparatively less. These studies have revealed the presence of a cognitive appraisal mechanism which allows evaluation of various aspects of the given environment by the person before he experiences stress.

It is evident that arousal of stress in high density and encroachment of personal space if attributed to the presence of others produces the feeling of crowding. Future research may show that under inevitable circumstances of high density and scarcity of resources (a) What other mechanisms individuals adopt to cope with these circumstances? (b) Whether a consideration of others' social values would still prevail in these situations? (c) With limited resources what can be done to reduce the adverse effects of crowding? Considerable theoretical insights into crowding and its consequences are available but research is now needed to deal with the practical questions. In this context a model has been proposed by the author (Jain, 1985; 1986; Jain and Misra, 1986) which incorporates the relevant antecedent conditions and moderators which seem to determine the experience of crowding and its consequences at different levels of an individual's functioning.

Crowding and Individuals' Functioning: A Theoretical Model

The feeling of crowding can be viewed as a psychological state contingent upon high population density, mediated by physical resources, tolerance, and coping strategies. This implies that there is a possibility of differences within a group in the feeling of crowding in a constant environment characterised by high population density. The proposed mediating variables critically shape the quality of crowding experiences which, in turn, have specific consequences for individuals at the three levels of functioning, i.e., personal, interpersonal and community. The personal consequences include life stresses, anxiety, withdrawal, health and personal control. These consequences relate the individual to his environment and have implications for the individual's growth. The consequences at the interpersonal level emphasise relationships with other individuals. However, three major consequences can be identified. They include social support, competition and affiliation. Finally, crowding has consequences at the community level which are related to participation in community activities.

It may be pointed out that the consequences of crowding at the three levels of an individual's functioning are not independent of each other. Experiences at any one of the three levels may increase or decrease the magnitude of effects at the other two levels. Also, these consequences provide feedback to the individual and contribute to the feeling of crowding. This framework does not preclude the existence of possible linkages between high population density and behavioural consequences. Under certain situations it is possible to have a direct relationship between high population density and an individual's functioning at the three levels. A model is graphically presented in the figure below.

The proposed model conceives the variables in the following manner.

Antecedent Conditions

POPULATION DENSITY: Population density is operationalised in terms of two objective indices, i.e., inside density (number of persons

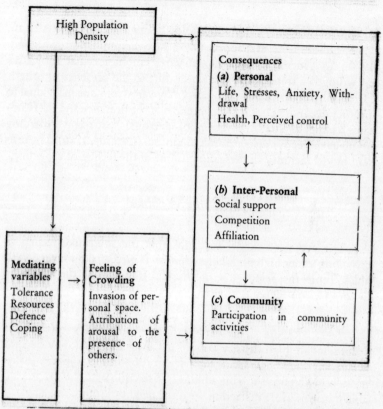

Figure: *Relationship between Crowding and an Individual's functioning*

per room, and room deficit) and a measure of outside density in the area. The number of rooms in the household can be regressed on the number of people in the household. Thus, the predicted number of rooms for a household of a given size and composition could be computed. The actual number of rooms in a household minus the number predicted for its size and composition is the room deficit score (Booth, 1976).

FEELING OF CROWDING: There is consensus among researchers that crowding deals with the subjective state which typically has a stress component. Some researchers have argued that such feelings are associated with perceptions of reduced physical or psychological space (Stokols, 1976). Others have emphasised the feeling of loss of control over interactions and excess contact with others (Altman, 1975; Desor, 1972; Rapaport, 1975), or overstimulation (Milgram, 1970). In general all these approaches emphasise that subjective crowding is a state of stress which is due to the presence of others. How many others will be tolerated may vary from one individual to another depending upon the awareness of the presence and the resultant feeling of stress. Invasion of personal space and crowding involves subjective discomfort and arousal (Lazarus, 1966). The present model includes all these dimensions of the feeling of crowding.

Mediating Variables

The proposed model contends that the subjective feeling of crowding under high population density is mediated by several variables. From the perspective of stressful transactions the following factors are considered relevant.

TOLERANCE: This refers to the individual's capacity to accommodate high density conditions. An individual may become accustomed and begin liking high density conditions. Operationally, it can be defined as showing a liking/satisfaction with the space available in the house, satisfaction with the neighbourhood and physical facilities available, and a desire to remain in the prevailing conditions.

RESOURCES: This category constitutes the physical resources and facilities available to the individual in the house as well as in the locality.

DEFENCE: In this context defence is considered as an effort aimed at protecting one's self from the interference created by the presence of others, both at the psychological as well as the physical levels. For example, constructing a high boundary wall around the house, or a partition wall to keep others out of vision, growing trees and fencing, keeping doors closed, may be considered as defences at the physical level. Similarly adopting such a time table in the family so that at any given time of the day all members of the family do not remain in the house, arranging the furniture in such a way that family members do not face each other as far as possible, are some instances of psychological defence. In fact the difference between physical and psychological defences is very little.

Since high density condition is characterised by the presence of many persons in a small space, the first and foremost implication of this situation is the unwanted interaction with others. Therefore, in order to cope with this situation social interactions should be managed in such a way as to reduce the amount of stress.

Consequences of Crowding

The present model includes the following variables as consequences of crowding at the personal, interpersonal, and community levels. Though these variables are mentioned independently, they are supposed to influence each other.

PERSONAL CONSEQUENCES: These include life stresses, anxiety, withdrawal, health and perceived control.

(a) *Life Stresses.* Since crowding has been considered as stress in itself, it is reasonable to believe that it would be related to other life stresses which most people face in day-to-day life. Crowding is supposed to intensify these stresses.

(b) *Anxiety.* Crowding has been reported to lower the threshold of anxiety producing situations. Accordingly, an attempt can be made to examine the levels of state anxiety as conceived by Mehrabian and Russell (1974). They have proposed that state anxiety involves low pleasure and low dominance with high arousal. Thus state anxiety is a feeling of having little pleasure rather displeasure and of limited freedom of choice with feeling excitement (too many stimuli to be attended or stimulus anxiety). These three components are independent in themselves but together their joint effect can be viewed as state anxiety.

(c) *Withdrawal.* Crowding may produce a tendency to withdraw from this unpleasant situation. This is manifested in planning to leave the crowded situation. In the present context, planning to leave the residence, expressed pleasure over the opportunity to change one's residence or town for a more spacious accommodation, the efforts on the part of the individual to stay in the house/locality for the shortest period, etc., are viewed as objective indicators of withdrawal.

(d) *Health.* The relationship of crowding with the status of mental and physical well being/ill health has been established in several studies. However, the findings have not always been consistent (e.g., Freedman, Heshka and Levy 1975). The differences may be partly attributable to the differences in the measures, e.g., blood pressure, medical history, and measures of mental and physical health. Thus psychological as well as physiological measures must be included to assess problems related to health.

(e) *Perceived Control.* In high density environments a loss of control over social interactions as well as outcomes is generally experienced. This loss of control is mainly because of reduced choices and lack of correspondence in the attempt to reduce the feelings of crowding and success in achieving that situation.

INTERPERSONAL CONSEQUENCES: These include competition, affiliation and social support.

(a) *Competition.* High population density creates competition for the utilisation of available resources (including spatial facilities). Competition involves a desire for acting alone to enjoy some facilities in or outside the home with a feeling that someone else may get the same if he misses the chance.

(b) *Affiliation.* A number of studies have documented that the need for affiliation is related to the experience of crowding. In the present model affiliation is viewed in terms of those social activities in which one participates, i.e., membership of various associations.

(c) *Social Support.* Prolonged living in a high density area or house may lead to adaptation to such situations. Those who develop adaptation might perceive the situation more positively. This positive perception may include the feeling of greater social support from the neighbourhood. In the course of their stay in high density areas people may develop an affinity with their neighbours and also experience a feeling of happiness being amongst those neighbours, and leaving them may be perceived as painful.

COMMUNITY CONSEQUENCES: This category includes community activities.

(a) *Community Activities.* These activities can be characterised as activities jointly undertaken by the community members. Neighbourhood, caste, or regional groups can be changed as a result of the feeling of crowding.

Crowding and Environmental Planning

The knowledge of crowding and its consequences for human behaviour is relevant to town-planners, policy-makers and educators in facilitating their role in developing human resources, maintaining and enhancing the positive features of the environment, and contributing to the quality of life. These aspects have largely been neglected for a long time because of lack of awareness as well as due to the implicit notion that people develop the desired environmental attitudes with increasing age, and it does not require any special instruction. However, the experience in the last few decades has shown that such an assumption is false. There has been a remarkable decline in the standards of living and rapid increase in environmental pollution. These trends are assuming alarming proportions and urgent measures are necessary for insuring provisions for a livable environment. The task is to develop a healthy and balanced attitude towards the individual-environment relationship. So far, the model of development considered environment as a resource to be exploited and man was central to all the developmental endeavours. This led to an attitude that environment is for the individual. This lop-sided assumption has superficially contributed to temporary advancements. The hidden costs of such efforts are now becoming apparent. Development is not a unitary concept. It has several facets and we have to select a model of development which is best suited to our culture, ethos, and environment.

Indian planners and policy-makers have not paid sufficient attention to the ill-effects of high population density. Their prime concern is implementing family planning programmes and have achieved considerable success in bringing down the rate of population growth. However, these efforts are not sufficient. Population is growing and, even at a reduced rate, is assuming unmanageable proportions. Some intellectuals have argued strongly in favour of alternative models of development. Recently, Gupte (1984) surveyed many cities of the world and reported on the plight of those who are living in crowded conditions. He concluded that 'on this crowded earth of ours, there is not just one population problem but many.... Population programme and policies must be tailored to suit a particular country, its culture and its specific needs and conditions' (p. 319).

The development of high technology and industrial growth have limited capacity to improve the quality of life when people are 'bursting into the cities partly in hope but always without sufficient skills or education' (Schneider, 1979, p. 272). These authors have recommended that Third World countries should not follow the Western model of development.

The model of development has to be changed as the current problems of population management are largely the outcome of the Western model of development. The Western model leads to prosperity but has harmful consequences for the quality of life. In American cities there is a growing alienation amongst the city dwellers living in well-planned houses which forces them into social exclusion in the name of privacy (Schneider, 1979).

Thus, we are caught in a trap, for if we build houses (if our economy permits) to reduce crowding we may be moving on the path towards alienation and if we do not build houses for the teeming millions we shall inevitably move towards the destruction of society. As Buch (1987) has noted 'the design, layout and construction of mass housing that there has been an almost total failure in India' (p. 165). Planning needs to be adopted to the Indian socio-cultural conditions.

The population explosion is not less frightening than the atomic explosion. The difference between the two may be considered in terms of time only. Both are poisonous: one is slow, the other is instantaneous. The horror of future population has to be controlled now through both family planning measures as well as regulation of the affairs of daily life. High density (which is inevitable with the population growth) adversely affects interpersonal interactions and mental health, and motivates the individual to develop competition tolerance and consequently changes the needs, increases hostility, yields poor performance on complex tasks, and increases the likelihood of illness. The individual in the scarcity of resources condition also feels stress similar to that experienced in a high density condition. The stress at the individual level is more likely to reflect at the social and community levels as envisaged in the proposed model. The effects of population density are quite similar in urban and rural areas. But so far its effects have not manifested themselves at the interpersonal level and in expected helping at least in a city having approximately one million population. But bigger cities like Bombay and Calcutta are most likely to yield adverse effects on interpersonal attraction and helping. American city-planners have suggested a possibility that rural people having close interpersonal bonds at the individual level may develop group bonds as they move from rural to urban settings and the group bonds in the midst of frustration may be expressed in tyrannous intent (Schneider, 1979).

Viewed in the context of developmental planning the problem of population growth and the management of its products have indicated the failure of the 'Catch up Model' which has been compelling developing countries like India to emulate the life and pattern of developed countries. As J.B.P. Sinha (1985) has diagnosed, development cannot be profitably internalised if it is not rooted in the indigenous cultural context. Development is primarily and ultimately related to the eco-cultural and social context of the country.

References

ABRAMSON, L.Y., M.E.P. SELIGMAN and J.D. TEASDALE 1978. Learned helplessness in humans: Critique and reformulations. *Journal of Abnormal Psychology, 87,* 49-74.

AIELLO, J.R. and A. BAUM. 1979. *Residential crowding and design.* New York: Plenum.

AIELLO, J.R., A. BAUM and F.P. GORMLEY. 1981. Social determinants of residential crowding stress. *Personality and Social Psychology Bulletin, 7* 643-49.

AIELLO, J.R. and L. CAPRIGLIONE. 1975. *Effects of crowding on the elderly.* Unpublished manuscript. Rutgers University.

AIELLO, J.R., D.T. DeRIST, Y.M. EPSTEIN and R.A. KARLIN. 1977. Crowding and the role of interpersonal distance preference. *Sociometry, 40,* 272-82.

AIELLO, J.R., Y. EPSTEIN, and R. KARLIN. 1975. *Field experimental research on human crowding.* Paper presented at the meeting of the Western Psychological Association, Sacramento, California, April 1975.

AIELLO, J.R., J.S. VAUTIER and M.D. BERNSTEIN. 1983. *Crowding stress: Impact of social support, group formation, and control.* Paper presented at the 91st Annual Convention of

American Psychological Association, Anaheim, California. August 1983.

ALTMAN, I. 1978. Crowding: Historical and contemporary trends in crowding research. In A. Baum and Y.M. Epstein eds., *Human response to crowding*. Hillsdale, N.J.: Earlbaum.

_____. 1975. *The environment and social behaviour.* Monterey, California: Brooks/Cole.

ALTMAN, I. and M.M. CHEMERS. 1980. Cultural aspects of environ-ment-behaviour relationships. In H. Triandis ed., *Handbook of cross cultural psychology*. Vol. 5. Boston: Allyn & Bacon.

ALTMAN, I. and A.M. VINSEL. 1977. Personal space: An analysis of E.T. Hall's proxemics framework. In I. Altman and J. Whol-will eds., *Human behaviour and environment: Advances in theory and research*. Vol. 2. New York: Plenum Press.

ANAND, M. 1983. *In dwelling and out dwelling experience of crowding and special cognitive and affective responses.* Unpublished master's dissertation. Allahabad University, Allahabad.

ARGYLE, M. and J. DEAN. 1965. Eye contact, distance and affiliation. *Sociometry, 28,* 289-304.

ATKINSON, J.W. 1958. *Motives in fantasy, action, and society.* Princeton, N.J.: Van Nostrand.

AVERILL, J.R. 1973. Personal control over aversive stimuli and its relationship to stress. *Psychological Bulletin, 80,* 286-303.

BAIN, S.M. 1974. A geographer's approach in the epidemiology of psychiatric disorder. *Journal of Biological Sciences, 6,* 195-220.

BALDASSARE, M. 1975. The effect of density on social behaviour and attitudes. *American Behavioral Scientist, 18,* 815-25.

BARON, R.M. and D.R. MENDEL. 1978. Toward an ecological model of density effects in dormitory settings. In A. Baum and Y.M. Epstein eas., *Human response to crowding.* Hillsdale, N.J.: Earlbaum.

BARON, R.M., D.R. MENDEL, C.A. ADAMS, and L.M. GRIFFEN. 1976. Effects of social density in university residential envi-ronments. *Journal of Personality and Social Psychology, 34,* 343-446.

BARON, R.M. and S.P. NEEDEL. 1980. Towards an understanding of the differences in the responses of humans and other animals to density. *Psychological Review, 87,* 320-26.

BARON, R.M. and J.RODIN. 1978. Personal controls mediator of crowding. In A. Baum, J.E. Singer and S. Valins eds., *Advances in environmental psychology*. Vol. 1. Hillsdale, N.J.: Earlbaum.

BARKER, R.G. 1965. Explorations in ecological psychology. *American Psychologist, 20,* 1-14.

_____. 1968. *Ecological psychology: Concepts and methods for studying the environment of human behaviour.* California: Stanford.

BASS, M.H. and M.S. WEINSTEIN. 1971. Early development of interpersonal distance in children. *Canadian Journal of Behavioral Science, 3,* 368-76.

BAUM, A., J.R. AIELLO and L.E. CALESNICK. 1978. Crowding and personal control: Social density and the development of learned helplessness. *Journal of Personality and Social Psychology, 36,* 1000-11.

BAUM, A. and G.E. DAVIS. 1976. Spatial and social aspects of crowding perception. *Environment and Behavior, 8,* 527-44.

BAUM, A., G.E. DAVIS, L.E. CALESNICK and R.J. GATHEL. 1982. Individual differences in coping with crowding: Stimulus screening and social overload. *Journal of Personality and Social Psychology, 43,* 821-30.

BAUM, A. and C.I. GREENBERG. 1975. Waiting for a crowd: The behavioral and perceptual effects of anticipated crowding. *Journal of Personality and Social Psychology, 32,* 671-67.

BAUM, A. and S. KOMAN. Differential response to anticipated crowding: Psychological effects of social and spatial density. *Journal of Personality and Social Psychology, 34,* 526-36.

BAUM, A., J.E. SINGER, and C.S. BAUM. 1981. Stress and the environment. *Journal of Social Issues, 37,* 4-35.

BAUM, A. and S. VALINS. 1977. *Associates: Architecture and social behaviour: Psychological studies of social density.* Hillsdale, N.J.: Earlbaum.

_____ 1979. Architectural mediation of residential density and control: Crowding and the regulation of social contact. In L. Berkowitz ed., *Advances in experimental social psychology*. Vol. 12. New York: Academic Press.

BERGMAN, B.A. 1971. The effects of group size, personal space, and success-failure on psychological arousal, test performance and questionnaire responses. *Dissertation Abstracts International, A* 2319-3420.

BERLYNE, D.E. 1960 *Conflict, curiosity and arousal.* New York: McGraw-Hill.

_____. 1967. Arousal and reinforcement. In D. Levine ed., *Nebraska symposium on motivation.* Nebraska: University of Nebraska Press.

_____. 1971. *Aesthetics and psychology.* New York: Appleton-Century-Crofts.

BOOTH, A. 1976. *Urban crowding and its consequences.* New York: Praeger.

BOOTH, A. and S. WELCH. 1974. Crowding and urban crime rates. Paper presented at the meeting of the Midwest Sociological Association, Omaha, Nebraska.

BRICKMAN, L., A. TEGER, T. GABRIELLE, C. MCLAUGHLIN, M. BERGER and E. SUNDAY. 1973. Dormitory density and helping behaviour. *Environment and Behavior, 5,* 465-89.

BROADBENT, D.E. 1971. *Decision and stress.* New York: Academic Press.

BROWN, L.R. (1979). *The twenty ninth day.* New Delhi: Radha Krishna Prakashan.

BRUCH, M.A. and J.L. WALKER. 1978. Effects of population density and information overload on state anxiety and crowding perception. *Psychological Records, 28,* 207-14.

BUCH, M.N. 1987. *Planning the Indian city.* New Delhi: Vikas Publishing House.

BURGER, J.M., J.A. OAKMAN and N.G. BULLARD. 1983. Desire for control and perception of crowding. *Personality and Social Psychology Bulletin, 9,* 475-79.

BYRNE, D. 1971. *The attraction paradigm.* New York: Academic Press.

BYRNE, D. and G.L. CLORE. 1970. A reinforcement model of evaluative responses. *Personality: An International Journal, 1,* 103-38.

CALHOUN, J.B. 1962. Population density and social pathology. *Scientific American, 206,* 49-59.

_____. 1971. Space and the strategy of life. In A.H. Esser ed., *Behavior and environment: The use of space by animals and men.* New York: Plenum Press.

_____. 1973. Death squared: The explosive growth and demise of a mouse population. Proceedings of the Royal Society of Medicine.

CANTER, D. and S. CANTER. 1971. Close together in Tokyo. *Design and Environment, 2,* 60-63.

CANTER, D. and I. GRIFFITHS, trs. 1982. Claude Levy-Leboyer, *Psychology and environment.* Beverley Hills: Sage Publications.

CARSON, D.H. 1969. Population, concentration and human stress. In B.P. Rourke ed., *Explorations in the psychology of stress and anxiety.* Don Mills, Canada: Longmans.

CARTER, L.J. 1969. The population crisis: Rising concern at home. *Science, 166,* 722-26.

CENSUS OF INDIA. 1981.

CHRISTIAN, J.J. 1955. Effect of population size on the adrenal glands and reproductive organs of male white mice. *American Journal of Physiology, 181,* 477-90.

_____. 1959. The role of endocrine and behavioral factors in the growth of mammalian population. In A. Gorbman ed., *Comparative endocrinology.* New York: Wiley.

_____. (1963). The pathology of over population. *Military Medicine, 128,* 571-603.

CHRISTIAN, J.J., V. FLYGER and D.E. DAVIS. 1960. Factors in the mass mortality of a herd of skia deer, *Cervus nippon. Chesapeake Science, 1,* 79-95.

COHEN, S. 1980. Aftereffects of stress on human performance and social behaviour: A review of research and theory. *Psychological Bulletin, 88,* 82-108.

_____. 1978. Environmental load and the allocation of attention. In A. Baum, J.Singer and Valins eds., *Advances in environmental psychology.* Vol. 1. Hillsdale, N.J.: Earlbaum.

COHEN, S., D.C. GLASS and S. PHILLIPS. 1979. Environment and health. In H.E. Freeman, S. Levine and L.G. Reeder eds., *Handbook of sociology.* Englewood Cliffs, N.J.: Prentice Hall.

COX, V., P.B. PAULUS and G. MCCAIN. 1984. Prison crowding research: The relevance for prison housing standard and a general approach regarding crowding phenomena. *American Psychologist, 39,* 1148-60.

COX, V.C., P.M. PAULUS, G. MCCAIN and M. KARLOVAC. 1982. The relationship between crowding and health. In A. Baum and J. Singer eds., *Advances in environmental psychology.* Hillsdale, N.J. : Earlbaum.

D'ARTI, D.A., E.F. FITZGERALD, S.V. KASL and A.M. OSTFELD. 1981. Crowding in prison: The relationship between changes in housing mode and blood pressure. *Psychosomatic Medicine, 43,* 95-105.

DARLEY, J. and B. LATANE. 1968. Bystander intervention in emergency: Diffusion of responsibility. *Journal of Personality and Social Psychology, 8,* 377-83.

DAVIS, D.E. 1971. Physiological effects of continued crowding. In A.H. Esser ed., *Behavior and environment: The use of space by animals and men.* New York: Plenum.

DESOR, J.A. 1972. Towards a psychological theory of crowding. *Journal of Personality and Social Psychology, 2,* 79-83.

DEUTSCH, M. 1953. The effects of cooperation and competition upon group process. In D. Cartwright and A. Zander eds., *Group dynamics.* New York: Harper and Row.

DOOLEY, B.B. 1974. Crowding stress: The effects of social density on men with 'close' or 'far' personal space. Unpublished doctoral dissertation. University of California.

DUBOS, R. 1965. *Man adapting.* New Haven, Conn: Yale University Press.

EDWARD, R and H. JACOB, 1975. Competition with oneself vs. others as a facilitator in the class room. *Journal of Social Psychology, 95,* 281-82.

EDWARDS, A.L. 1954. *Personal preference schedule manual.* Agra: The Psychological Corporation.

EOYANG, C.K. 1974. Effects of group size and privacy in residential crowding. *Journal of Personality and Social Psychology, 30,* 389-92.

EPSTEIN, Y.M. and R.A. KARLIN. 1975. Effects of acute experimental crowding. *Journal of Applied Social Psychology, 4,* 34-53.

EVANS, G.W. 1978. Human spatial behavior: The arousal model. In A. Baum and Y.M. Epstein eds., *Human response to crowding.* Hillsdale, N.J. : Earlbaum.

FACTOR, R. and I. WALDRON. 1973. Contemporary population density and human health. *Nature, 243,* 381-84.

FAGOT, B.I. and G.R. PATTERSON. 1969. An In-vivo analysis of reinforcing contingencies for sex role behaviors in the preschool child. *Developmental Psychology, 1,* 563-68.

FAWCETT, J.T. 1970. *Psychology and population.* An occasional paper of the Population Council.

FESTINGER, L., S. SCHACHTER and K. BACK. 1950. *Social pressures in informal groups: A study of human factors in housing.* Stanford, California: Stanford University.

FOWLER, H. 1970. Implications of sensory reinforcement. In R. Glasser ed., *The nature of reinforcement.* New York: Associate Press.

FOX, R.G. 1975. Competitive modernization. In H.E. Ullrich ed., *Competition and modernisation in South Asia.* New Delhi: Abhinav Publications.

FREEDMAN, J.L. 1972. The effects of population density on humans. In J. Fawcett ed., *Psychological perspective on population.* New York: Basic Books.

_____ 1975. *Crowding and behavior.* San Francisco: Freeman.

_____ 1979. Reconciling apparent differences between the responses of human and other animals to crowding. *Psychological Review, 86,* 80-85.

FREEDMAN, J.L., J. BRISKY, and A. CAVOUKIAN. 1980. Environmental determinants of behavioral contagion: Density and number. *Basic and Applied Social Psychology, 1,* 155-61.

FREEDMAN, J.L., S. HESHKA, and A. LEVY. 1975. Crowding as an intensifier of pleasantness and unpleasantness. In J.L. Freedman ed., *Crowding and behavior.* San Francisco: Freeman.

FREEDMAN, J.L., S. KLEVANSKY, and P.R. EHRLICH. 1971. The effects of crowding on human task performance. *Journal of Applied Social Psychology, 1,* 7-25.

FREEDMAN, J.L., A.S. LEVY, R.W. BUCHANAN and J. PRICE, 1972. Crowding and human aggressiveness. *Journal of Experimental Social Psychology, 8,* 528-48.

FREEMAN, F. 1965. *Theory and practice of psychological testing.* New Delhi: Oxford & I.B.H. Publishing.

GAHLOT, P.S., S. GAUTAM, and S.D. GUPTA. 1983. Epidemiological study of mental illness in a migrant urban population. Project Report of the Indian Council of Medical Research, Psychiatric Centre, Jaipur.

GALLE, O.R., W.R. GOVE, J.M. MCPHERSON. 1972. Population density and pathology: What are the relations for man? *Science, 176,* 23-30.

GANGULI, B.N. 1974. The future quality of population. In A. Bose, P. Desai, A. Mitra, and J. Sharma eds., *Population in India's Development.* New Delhi: Vikas Publishing House.

GIBSON, J.J. 1977. Theory of affordance. In R.E. Shaw and J. Bransford eds., *Perceiving, acting and knowing: Toward an ecological psychology.* Hillsdale, N.J.: Earlbaum.

GLASS, D.C. and J.E. SINGER. 1972. *Urban stress.* New York: Academic Press.

GOECKNER, D.F., W.T. GREENOUGH and W.R. MEAD. 1973. Deficits in learning tasks following chronic overcrowding in rats. *Journal of Personality and Social Psychology, 28,* 256-61.

GOLSON, H.L. 1976. Crowding, social structure, and pathology in cities. *Dissertation Abstracts International, 37,* 5322.

GORMLY, J., A. GORMLY and C. JOHNSON. 1971. Interpersonal attraction: Competence, motivation, and reinforcement theory. *Journal of Personality and Social Psychology, 19,* 375-80.

GOVE, W.R., M. HUGHES and O.R. GALLE. 1979. Overcrowding in home. An empirical investigation of its possible pathological consequences. *American Sociological Review, 44,* 59-80.

GRIFFITT, W. and R. VEITCH. 1971. Hot and crowded: Influence of population density and temperature on interpersonal behavior. *Journal of Personality and Social Psychology, 17,* 92-98.

GUPTE, P. 1984. *The crowded earth.* New York: Norton.

HALL, E.T. 1966. *The hidden dimension.* New York: Doubleday.

HAWANG, K.K. 1979. Coping with residential crowding in a Chinese urban society: The interplay of high density dwelling and interpersonal values. *Acta Psychologica Taiwanica, 21,* 47-124.

HAYDUCK, L.A. 1983. Personal space: Where we now stand? *Psychological Bulletin, 94,* 293-335.

HEBB, D.O. 1972. *Textbook of psychology.* Philadelphia: W.B. Saunders.

HEIMSTRA, N.W. and A.L. MCDONALD. 1973. The problem of overcrowding. In N.W. Heimstra and A.L. McDonald eds., *Psychology and contemporary problems.* Monterey, California: Brooks/Cole.

HOMANS, G. 1950. *The human group.* New York: Harcourt Brace.

HORNEY, K. 1939. *New ways in psychoanalysis*. New York: Norton.

HOROWITZ, M.J., D.J. DUTT, and L.O. STRATLON. Personal space and the body-buffer zone. *Archives of General Psychiatry*, *11*, 651-56.

HOUSE, J.S. and S. WOLF. 1978. Effects of urban residence on interpersonal trust and helping behavior. *Journal of Personality and Social Psychology*, *36*, 1024-43.

HUTT, C. and M. VAIZEY. 1966. Differential effects of group density on social behaviour. *Nature*, *209*, 1371-72.

IWATA, D. 1979. Selected personality traits as determinants of perception of crowding. *Japanese Psychological Research*, *21*, 1-9.

JAIN, U. 1976. Competition tolerance and need hierarchy pattern as related to population growth. Project report of the Indian Council of Social Science Research.

_____. 1978. Competition tolerance in high-low density urban-rural areas. *Journal of Social Psychology*, *105*, 297-98.

_____. Effect of population density on human social behaviour and coping in dense environment. Project report of the Indian Council of Social Science Research.

_____. 1984. Effect of inside-outside density on social behaviour. Paper presented at U.G.C. Workshop. Jaipur: University of Rajasthan.

_____. 1985. High population density and human behaviour. Paper presented at the U.G.C. National Seminar on Environmental Psychology. University of Rajasthan, Jaipur, March 1985.

_____. 1987. Effect of Population density and resources on the feeling of crowding and personal space. *Journal of Social Psychology*, *27*, 331-38.

JAIN, U. and G. MISRA. 1986. Consequences of crowding. Paper presented at the workshop on Population Education. Regional College of Education, Bhopal, July 1986.

JAIN, U., and SURAJMAL. 1983. Effect of prolonged deprivation on attribution of causes of success and failure. *Journal of Social Psychology*, *124*, 143-49.

KAHNEMAN, D. 1973. *Attention and effort*. Englewood Cliffs, N.J.: Prentice Hall.

KANNAMPUZHA, G.J. 1976. *The crowding phenomenon: Psychological perspective.* Paper presented at the All India Interdisciplinary Seminar on Human Settlements. Jaipur: University of Rajasthan.

KARLIN, R.A. and Y.M. EPSTEIN. 1979. Acute crowding: A reliable method for inducing stress in humans. *Research Communication in Psychology, Psychiatry, and Behaviour, 4,* 357-70.

KIRMEYER, S. 1978. Urban density and pathology: A review of research. *Environment and behavior, 10,* 249-69.

KLIEN, K. and B. HARRIS. 1979. Disruptive effects of disconfirmed expectancies about crowding. *Journal of Personality and Social Psychology, 37,* 669-77.

KONECNI, V.J., L. LIBUSER, H. MORTON, and E.B. EBBESEN. 1975. Effects of violation of personal space on escape and helping responses. *Journal of Experimental Social Psychology, 11,* 288-99.

KORTE, C. and N. KERR. 1975. Responses to altruistic opportunities under urban and rural conditions. *Journal of Social Psychology, 95,* 183-84.

KULKARNI, K.M. 1984. *Geography of crowding and human response.* New Delhi: Concept Publishers.

LANGER, E.J. and S. SAEGART. 1977. Crowding and cognitive control. *Journal of Personality and Social Psychology, 35,* 175-82.

LAVIN, M.W. 1983. Territoriality and privacy regulation in shared residential spaces. Paper presented at the 91st annual convention of the American Psychological Association, Anaheim, California, August 1983.

LAZARUS, R.S. 1966. *Psychological stress and the coping process.* New York: McGraw-Hill.

_____. 1974. *The riddle of man.* Englewood Cliffs, N.J.: Prentice-Hall.

LAZARUS, R.S. and COHEN, J.B. 1977. Environmental Stress. In I. Altman and J. Wohlwill eds., *Human behavior and environment.* Vol. 2. New York: Plenum Press.

LAZARUS, R.S. and S. FOLKMAN. 1984. *Stress appraisal and coping.* New York: Springer.

LEVY, L. and A.N. HERZOG. 1974. Effects of population density and crowding on health and social adaptation in the Netherlands. *Journal of Health and Social Behavior, 15,* 228-40.

LOO, C. 1972. The effects of spatial density on the social behavior of children. *Journal of Applied Social Psychology, 2,* 372-81.

MARSHALL, J.E. and R. HESLIN. 1975. Boys and girls together:

Sexual composition and the effect of density and group size on cohesiveness. *Journal of Personality and Social Psychology, 31,* 952-61.

MASLOW, A.H. 1962. *Towards a psychology of being.* Englewood Cliffs, N.J.: Prentice Hall.

MCCAIN, G., V.C. COX and P.B. PAULUS. 1980. *The effect of prison crowding on inmate behavior.* Washington, D.C.: National Institute of Justice.

MCCAIN, G., V.C. COX, P.B. PAULUS, A. LUKE and H. ABADZI. 1985. *Journal of Applied Social Psychology, 15,* 503-15.

MCCALLUM, R., C.E. RUSBULT, G.K. HONG, T.A. WALDEN and J. SCHOPLER. 1979. Effects of resource availability and importance of behavior on the experience of crowding. *Journal of Personality and Social Psychology, 37,* 304-13.

MCCLELLAND, L.A. 1974. Crowding and social stress. Unpublished doctoral dissertation. University of Michigan.

MCCLELLAND, D.C., J.W. ATKINSON, A.A. CLARK and F.L. LOWELL. 1953. *The achievement motive.* New York: Appleton-Century-Crofts.

MCGGREW, P.L. 1970. Social and spatial density effects on spacing behavior in pre-school children. *Journal of Child Psychology and Psychiatry, 11,* 197-205.

MCGUIRE, J.M. and M.H. THOMAS. 1975. Effects of sex, competence, and competition on sharing behavior in children. *Journal of Personality and Social Psychology, 32,* 490-94.

MEAD, M. 1961. *Cooperation and competition among primitive peoples.* Boston: The Beacon Press.

MEHRABIAN, A. and J.A. RUSSELL. 1974. *An approach to environmental psychology.* Boston, Mass.: The MIT Press.

MILGRAM, S. 1970. The experience of living in cities. *Science, 167,* 1461-68.

MISRA, G. and A. SHUKLA. 1986. Environmental characteristics and the development of spatial representation in children. *Psychologia, 29,* 115-22.

MISRA, G. and L.B. TRIPATHI. 1978. Prolonged deprivation and status perception. *Indian Journal of Social Work, 39,* 113-21.

MITCHEL, R.E. 1971. Some social implications of high density housing. *American Sociological Review, 36,* 18-28.

MUNROE, R.L. and R.H. MUNROE. 1972. Population density and affective relationships in three East African societies. *Journal of Social Psychology, 88,* 15-20.

MURRAY, H.A. 1962. *Explorations in personality.* New York: Science Editions. Originally published in 1938.

MYERS, A. 1962. Team composition, success, and the adjustment of group members. *Journal of Abnormal and Social Psychology*, 325-32.

NAGAR, D. 1985. Experience and consequences of crowding. Unpublished doctoral dissertation. Allahabad University, Allahabad.

OKUM, M.A. and N.D. VESTA. 1975. Cooperation and competition in coaching groups. *Journal of Personality and Social Psychology*, *31*, 615-20.

PANDEY, J. 1978. Effects of crowding on human social behaviour. *Journal of Social and Economic Studies*, *5*, 85-95.

PATTERSON, H.L. 1973. Compensation in nonverbal immediacy behaviors: A review. *Sociometry*, *36*, 237-52.

PAULUS, P.B. 1980. Crowding. In P.B. Paulus ed., *Psychology of group influence*. Hillsdale, N.J.: Earlbaum.

PAULUS, P.B. and R.W. MATTHEWS. 1980. When density affects task performance. *Personality and Social Psychology Bulletin*, *6*, 119-24.

PAULUS, P.B., G. McCAIN and V.C. COX. 1978. Death rates, psychiatric commitments, blood pressure, and perceived crowding as a function of institutional crowding. *Environmental Psychology and Non-Verbal Behavior*, *3*, 107-16.

PETTIGREW, T.F. 1967. Social evaluation theory: Convergences and applications. In D.Levine ed., *Nebraska symposium on motivation*. Nebraska: University of Nebraska Press.

PREET, K. and U. JAIN. 1984. Effects of population density on mental health. Paper presented at the Indian Psychiatric Conference, Udaipur, Rajasthan, December 1984.

_____. 1986. Altruism in urban and rural environment. Unpublished research paper. Rajasthan University, Jaipur.

PRICE, J. 1971. The effect of crowding on the social behavior of children. Unpublished doctoral dissertation. Columbia University, Ithaca.

PROSHANSKY, H.M. 1973. The environmental crisis in human dignity. *Journal of Social Issues*, *29*.

PROSHANSKY, H., W.H. ITTELSON, and L.G. RIVLIN eds., *Environmental psychology*. New York: Holt Rinehart and Winston.

RABBIE, J.M., F. BENOIST, H. OOSTERBAAN and L. VISSER. 1974. Differential power and effects of expected competitive and cooperative intergroup interaction on intergroup and outgroup attitude. *Journal of Personality and Social Psychology, 30,* 46-56.

RAGHAVACHARI, S. 1974. Population projections, 1976-2001. In A.Bose, A.Mitra, P.Desai and J.Sharma eds., *Population in India's development.* New Delhi: Vikas Publishing House.

RAPAPORT, A. 1975. Toward a redefinition of density. *Environment and Behavior, 7,* 133-58.

RAWLS, J.R., R.E. TREGO, C.N. MCGAFFERY, and D.J. RAWLS. 1972. Personal space as a predictor of performance, under close working conditions. *Journal of Social Psychology, 86,* 261-67.

RICHARD, W.B. 1977. The effects of anxiety on perceptions of crowding. *Dissertation Abstracts International, 38,* 3083.

RODIN, J. 1976. Density, perceived choice, and response to controllable and uncontrollable outcomes. *Journal of Experimental Social Psychology, 12,* 564-78.

RODIN, J. and A. BAUM. 1978. Potential consequences of density and loss of control. In A.Baum and Y.M. Epstein eds., *Human response to crowding.* Hillsdale, N.J.: Earlbaum.

ROHE, W. and A.H. PATTERSON. 1974. The effects of varied levels of resources and density on behavior in a day care center. Paper presented at the meeting of the Environmental Design Research Association, Milwaukee, Wisconsin, April 1974.

ROSEN, B.C. 1956. The achievement syndrome: A psychocultural dimension of social stratification. *American Sociological Review, 21,* 203-11.

RUBACK, R.B. and T.S. CARR. 1984. Crowding in women's prison: Attitudinal and behavioral effects. *Journal of Applied Social Psychology, 14,* 57-58.

SAEGERT, S. 1978. High density environments: Their personal and social consequences. In A.Baum and Y.M.Epstein eds., *Human response to crowding.* Hillsdale, N.J.: Earlbaum.

_____. 1973. Crowding: Cognitive overload and behavioral constraint. In W.Preiser, ed., *Environmental design research.* Vol.II. Stroudsburg, Pa: Dowden, Hutchinson and Ross.

_____. 1974. Effect of spatial and social density on arousal, mood, and social orientation. Unpublished doctoral dissertation. University of Michigan, Ann Arbor.

SCHMIDT, D.E. 1983. Personal control and crowding stress: A test of similarity in two cultures. *Journal of Cross-Cultural Psychology, 14,* 221-39.

SCHMIDT, D.E. and J.P. KEATING. 1979. Human crowding and personal control: An integration of the research. *Psychological Bulletin, 86,* 680-700.

SCHNEIDER, K.R. 1979. *On the nature of cities.* San Francisco: Jossey-Bass Publishers.

SCOTT, W.E. JR and CHERRINGTON. 1974. Effects of competitive and individualistic reinforcement contingencies. *Journal of Personality and Social Psychology, 30,* 748-58.

SELIGMAN, M.P. 1975. *Helplessness: On depression, development and death.* San Francisco: Freeman.

SELYE, H. 1976. *Stress in health and disease.* Woburn, Mass: Butterworth.

SENGAL, R.A. 1977. A systems analysis of population density and social pathology. *Dissertation Abstracts International, 37,* 5003.

SHAW, J.I. 1971. Situational factors contributing to a psychological advantage in competitive negotiations. *Journal of Personality and Social Psychology, 19,* 251-60.

SHERROD, D.R. 1974. Crowding, perceived control, and behavioral after effects. *Journal of Applied Social Psychology, 4,* 171-36.

SINHA, D. 1969. *Motivation of rural population in a developing country.* New Delhi: Allied Publishers.

_____. 1977. Some social disadvantages and development of certain perceptual skills. *Indian Journal of Psychology, 52,* 115-52.

SINHA, J.B.P. 1968. The construct of dependence proneness. *Journal of Social Psychology, 76,* 123-24.

_____. 1970. *Development through behaviour modification.* Bombay: Allied Publishers.

_____. 1985. Collectivism, social energy, and development in India. In A.R.Langunes and Y.H.Poortinga eds., *From different perspectives: Studies of behaviour across cultures.* Lisse: Swets and Zeitlinger.

SNYDER, R. 1961. Evolution and integration of mechanisms that regulate population growth. *Proceedings of the National Academy of Sciences, 47,* 449-55.

SOMMER, R. 1969. *Personal space: The behavioral basis of design.* Englewood Cliffs, N.J.: Prentice Hall.

STOKOLS, D. 1972. A social psychological model of human crowding phenomena. *Journal of the American Institute of Planners, 38,* 72-84.

_____. 1976. The experience of crowding in primary and secondary environments. *Environment and Behavior, 8,* 49-86.

_____. 1978 a. A typology of crowding experience. In A Baum and Y.M.Epstein eds., *Human response to crowding.* Hillsdale, N.J.: Earlbaum.

_____. 1978 b. Environmental psychology. *Annual Review of Psychology, 29,* 253-95.

STOKOLS, D., M. RALL, B. PINNER, and J. SCHOPLER. 1973. Physical, social and personal determinants of the perception of crowding. *Environment and Behavior, 5,* 87-115.

SUNDSTROM, E. 1975. Toward an interpersonal model of crowding. *Sociological Symposium, 14,* 129-44.

_____. 1978. Crowding as a sequential process: Review of research on the effects of population density on humans. In A.Baum and Y.M.Epstein eds., *Human response to crowding.* Hillsdale, N.J.: Earlbaum.

SWAMY, S. 1974. Population growth and economic development. In A.Bose, P.Desai, A.Mitra and J.Sharma eds., *Population in India's development.* New Delhi: Vikas Publishing House.

TENNIS, G.H. and J.M.DABBAS JR.1975. Sex, setting, and personal space. First grade through college. *Sociometry, 38,* 385-94.

TOFFLER, A. 1970. *The future shock.* New York: Bantam Books.

TRIPATHI, S. 1986. Effect of crowding on human behaviour. Unpublished doctoral dissertation. Kashi Vidyapeeth Varanasi.

TUCKER, J. and S.T. FRIEDMAN. 1972.Population density and group size. *American Journal of Sociology, 77,* 742-49

UNITED NATIONS. 1968. *Urbanization: Development policies and planning.* No. E. 68, IV. 1. New York: UN.

VALINS, S. and A. BAUM 1973. Residential group sizes, social interaction, and crowding. *Environment and Behavior, 5,* 421-39.

VAN STADEN, F.J. 1984. Developments in defining the experience of crowding. *South African Journal of Psychology, 14,* 20-22.

VEITCH, R., A. GESTINGER and D. ARKKALIN. 1976. A note on the reliability and validity of the CID scale. *The Journal of Psychology, 84,* 163-65.

WEINER, F.H. 1976. Altruism, ambience, and action: The effects of rural and urban rearing on helping behaviour. *Journal of Personality and Social Psychology, 34,* 112-24.

WHYTE, W.H. JR. 1956. *The organization man.* New York: Simon and Schuster.

WICKER, A.W. and S. KIRMEYER. 1977. From church to laboratory to national park: A program of research on excess and insufficient populations in behavior settings. In D.Stokols ed., *Psychological perspectives on environment and behavior: Conceptual and empirical trends.* New York: Plenum Press.

WINSBOROUGH, H. 1965. The social consequences of high population density. *Law and Contemporary Problems, 30,* 120-26.

WOLFE, M. 1975. Room size, group size, and density. *Environment and Behavior, 1,* 199-224.

WORCHEL, S. 1978. The experience of crowding: An attributional analysis. In A.Baum and Y.M.Epstein eds., *Human response to crowding.* Hillsdale, N.J.:Earlbaum.

WORCHEL, S., E. BROWN and W. WEBB. 1983. The influence of environmental control on attributing internal states. Paper presented at the 91st annual convention of the American Psychological Association, Anaheim, California, August 1983.

WORCHEL, S. and C. TEDDLIE. 1976. The experience of crowding: A two factor theory. *Journal of Personality and Social Psychology, 15,* 91-104.

WORCHEL, S. and S. YOHAI. 1979. The role of attribution in the experience of crowding. *Journal of Experimental Social Psychology, 15,* 91-104.

ZEEDYK-RYAN, J. and G.P. SMITH. 1983. The effects of crowding on hostility, anxiety, and desire for social interaction. *Journal of Social Psychology, 120,* 245-52.

ZLUTNICK, S. and I. ALTMAN. 1972. Crowding and human behavior. In J.Wohlwill and D.Carson eds., *Environment and the social sciences.* Washington, D.C.: American Psychological Association.

Author Index